ADVANCE COPY

This copy is an LIMITED ADVANCE COPY with less than 50 copies printed
There may be errors in typing, editing, writing, dates, times, spelling, punctuation, etc.
Read this book with the understanding that this is
not the final edited, copy edited, and proofread version.

ADVANCE COPY

This copy is a LIMITED ADVANCE COPY, with less than 50 copies printed
There may be errors in typing, editing, writing, dates, times, spelling, punctuation, etc.
Read this book with the understanding that this is
not the final edited, copy edited, and proofread version.

Written by Mannie L. Jackson

with Dreams to Reality Workbook
by Deborah S. Nelson

Boxcar Dreams Boardroom Reality
Dreams to Reality Workbook

www.BoxcarDreams.com

Copyright © 2011 by the authors of this book, Deborah S. Nelson & Mannie Jackson. The book authors retains sole copyright to contributions to this book.

Cover/book design by Deborah S. Nelson.

The interactive goal setting teaching model introduced in this series is patent pending; and may not be used without permission or a licensing agreement from Author Your Dreams Publishing Company.

Published by Author Your Dreams Publishing Company, 4419 Centennial Boulevard #390, Colorado Springs, CO 80907, info@AuthorYourDreams.com, www.BoxcarDreams.com

All Rights Reserved
No part of this book may be reproduced or used in any form without permission from the publisher. The original purchaser is hereby granted permission to print the pages for personal use.

Copies of this may NOT be transmitted, stored, or recorded in any form without written permission from the publisher, Author Your Dreams Publishing Company, who will prosecute any violations of copyright law, including e-mail attachments or any other means.

Forward

I have known Mannie Jackson for more than 36 years and married to him for 32 years. We have two beautiful daughters and a fairy tale rollercoaster life that never lacks excitement or surprises. As you may well imagine, I have had many memorable "Mannie moments" aside from the birth of our children, beginning with the courage he took to speak out for gays, lesbians, and transsexuals while at Honeywell and eventually chairing a regional task force to influence corporate and political policies and rights for domestic partnerships. Later in 2002, when I was at his side and he was blessed by Pope John Paul II before 85,000 people at the Vatican in Rome, Italy. Earlier we had journeyed to South Africa and I watched a human rights and corporate finance discussion between he and Nelson Mandela. And in 2009, watching and listening to him giving the commencement speech and receiving an Honorary Doctorate degree at his alma mater, the University of Illinois. I know how much he loved Illinois and how hard he worked to reach this point in his life and how much this opportunity meant to him.

I remember all the accomplishments and all the highs-and-lows, and there have been many; both personal and professional. At this stage of my life, I now only allow myself to recall the good times, and the many people along the way and particularly at Honeywell. I remember and think of the NBA bid in San Diego in 1989 and Mannie's ability to get meetings with the mayor, the NBA commissioner, and cabinet members in Washington D.C. and nearly succeed in achieving a bid for an NBA expansion Franchise with over 10,000 season ticket holders cheering his investment group's effort and supporting him.

Also, I think of countless hours of preparations for the Harlem Globetrotter acquisition, while balancing his family life, and a demanding executive position with Honeywell as well as all the charitable work he did for the Minneapolis community. He was so driven--it was contagious. He and I typed, sorted, organized, and brainstormed investor strategies, team improvement plans, and plans for making the workplace better for the players and employees, along with plans for initiating new charitable programs. After receiving input from staff members and various educators and consultants I finally saw his personal design of the first ever Globetrotter mascot, the wildly popular Globie came to fruition--all mascot designs and intent statements were complete over a holiday weekend, and focused entirely on education and entertaining children who would come to see the team perform.

Mannie has the best of intentions always--both in private moments and publicly. The reason he succeeds is that his stamina and commitment to task never waivers; he knows what he wants, he knows what is right and does what is right. He is generous, caring and brilliant. His leadership record at every stage of his life has allowed him to reach for the stars and follow his dreams. Mannie began work on this story about his Boxcar to Boardroom life over 15 year ago and I am as anxious as everyone else to

read and learn from his life and his opinions. Self told stories often come off egotistical and often will insult people mentioned or not mentioned. I believe this is one of the many reasons it's taken so long for him to get it right and with maximum positive impact.

This personal development book is an easy read case study in an educational format. In 1992, Mannie consulted with his friend Tom Cushman, a San Diego Sports writer to help in getting his story told and for reasons unknown to any of us at the time he stopped work on that book and put it away. He said he just didn't want to do a rags-to-riches story, in the context of sports or racial hardships, about his life.

My cousin Deborah Nelson sat down with Mannie one evening and began sharing stories about the subconscious commonalities of people who move forward in life against great odds. When Mannie discovered that success techniques could be taught and behaviors and priorities influenced through dream listening, he began immediately writing this book in cooperation with Deborah and now calls her his DREAM guru. Because he is both a believer and long-time practitioner in Dream listening, I truly believe you will enjoy your time spent with Mannie and Deborah. All of their work is done from the heart.

Catherine P Jackson

Preface

I've known Mannie for over 40 years – in my view his achievements rank him as a celebrity in contemporary society and an authentic pioneer and super star; he rose from impoverished means to become one of the wealthiest and most philanthropic African-Americans that survived pre-civil rights apartheid and poverty. Mannie is clearly a driven person with a deceptively brilliant mind and a quick study; and blessed with uncanny social skills to adapt and quickly assume leadership.

His role models were not movie stars, sports heroes, or media moguls; he often gives speeches about how he studied, learned from and emulated the style of great leaders from Franklin D. Roosevelt, to John F. Kennedy, Lee Iacocca, Phil Jackson, Martin Luther King, Barry Rand, Reebok's past CEO Paul Fireman, Ed Spencer, Bill Gates, George Bush Sr., Jesse Jackson, Jack Welch, Marian Wright Edelman, President Barrack and Michelle Obama, Maya Angelou, Barry Gordy, Bill Cosby, Abe Saperstein, Ronald Reagan, Jimmy Carter, Harry Truman, David Stern, Dennis Swanson (discovered Oprah and later spear-headed ESPN and their Wide World of Sports efforts), Hall of Famer Magic Johnson, Prince Charles, Ed Hightower, Pope John Paul, the Dali Lama, Winston Churchill, Hilary and Bill Clinton, Colin Powell, Nelson Mandela, Coach Joe Lucco, Jim Kaiser, Al Martins, Hazel O'Leary, Former U of I President Joe White, Reggie Lewis (of Beatrice Food fame), Oprah, Jerry Colangelo, Earl Graves, Robert "Bob" Johnson, Percy Sutton, Russell Simmons, CC Jones, Malcolm X, etc. to name just a few from all walks of life that he frequently quotes and speaks of with great admiration.

Most of these people he's worked with and/or knows on a first name basis. Each person on Mannie's personal leadership list he would say had great meaning in his life and inspired him and others to work harder than they ever dreamed to set and achieve important goals. I got to know Mannie when he worked for Honeywell (check the records, he is immortalized in their 100th anniversary history book) and later knew him as a racial pioneer when he was a President and a co-founder of ELC, a powerful network of Black Corp Executives. He is recognized as a business leader who was known as an exceptional marketing and strategic thinker, as an historic sports executive (the first black to own outright a major global sports Brand), as a board member who served on six fortune 500 boards and several non-profit boards, on one of which we served together, and as a man who received numerous awards including Hall of Fame recognition and two Honorary Doctorate degrees.

Despite all the promotions, award ceremonies, public appearances, high level negotiations and first name relationships with influential people, after his second goodwill trip to Iraq, he said that he wished he could do more toward achieving his lofty dreams and was apologizing for being too

reclusive and shy. And later was heard saying, "if it were not for the constant dreams of achievement, my compulsive need to engage myself in projects, the inspiration of his children, and the obligation he feels to his hometown of Edwardsville, Illinois; he could be very happy on an island somewhere in the Caribbean."

I often think about Mannie's heroics on the basketball court, in boardrooms, and the scores of countries he's visited and worked in and the thousands of people he knows. Six months ago I found myself, a lifetime public servant, very curious to read his books on any subject, whether it be sports, race relations, marketing, leadership, entrepreneurship, public policy, the Harlem Globetrotters, and especially what makes him "tick." Think about this, if you would – what drives a man to wake up at age 50 from an uncompensated dream and declares after 15 years away from the game and at just 6'2", 190 pounds, he wants to win a slam dunk contest, and to everyone's shock but his wife Cathy, he became so driven and committed to this dream he just got it done. I'm certain you'll enjoy Mannie's unique way of telling his stories as much as I did.

Anonymous

Mannie Jackson is the perfect guide to teach us how to convert our dreams into reality. Like President Lincoln and so many other Americans who rose high from humble beginnings, Mannie has been there, done that, and now tells us how we can do it too. Mannie is one of the finest men I've ever met. He has great character, integrity, presence and humility. We're lucky to have him as our teacher.

Mannie dreamed big, becoming an All-American basketball player and fine student at the University of Illinois. He worked hard and learned from others, including the legendary Abe Saperstein, owner of the Harlem Globetrotters. He extended respect to everyone as he built a great executive career at Honeywell, bought and revitalized the Harlem Globetrotters, and served many non-profit organizations including the University of Illinois and the Naismith Memorial Basketball Hall of Fame. Mannie has been true to his parents' guidance and values, loyal to the community where he grew up and generous to so many. Most important, Mannie has always defined for himself who he is and what matters to him. He wants others to have the satisfaction of the success and achievement he has earned. I hope you'll follow in his path!

B. Joseph White
President Emeritus, University of Illinois
Stephen M. Towey Professor of Business Leadership
College of Business
University of Illinois at Urbana-Champaign

My parents migrated to Edwardsville from Crawford and Brooksville, MS in the winter of 1942. I came to Edwardsville in the summer of 1944. I enrolled in and attended the all-black Lincoln School that fall. Both Mannie and I attended Lincoln School from the first grade through the seventh.

Academics were taught at Lincoln School, but we soon ascertained that the curriculums were separate form white schools and light years away from being equal. We looked forward to recess and lunchtime so that we could play games. Kickball and dodge ball were the "athletic" events and the flavor of the day. Lincoln had a "varsity" basketball team that consisted of the "upperclassmen," the 10th, 11th, and 12th graders. So there were no sports teams for those under 14 or 15 years old – whatever sports development we got – we got on our own.

When the schools integrated, Mannie and I had classes together – namely literature and social studies – as some of the terms and words were thrown our way, Mannie and I answered them gracefully and intelligently. On the basketball team, Mannie and Sam Johnson were on the starting five. Sam was a muscle player while Mannie was smooth, quick, and a fantastic leaper. He soon reached the plateau of being an excellent scorer and shooter. Our team went 16-0 that season.

Basketball and athletics came to the forefront in Mannie's and my life. Mannie had stated prior to going to high school that he was going to make the varsity basketball team as a freshmen. He did. We finished high school with honors and the satisfaction of playing on a championship caliber team. Our friendship became folklore as did our basketball accomplishments.

Mannie and I were granted four-year athletic scholarships to the University of Illinois. We were serious, focused, dedicated and roommates for four years. We both made the starting five and we started every game during our sophomore, junior, and senior years at the U of I. Freshmen were not allowed to play "upperclassmen" basketball during our tenure in college. We had excelled at the U of I and graduated within the allotted four years.

Mannie and I were the first two African-Americans to letter in varsity basketball at the U of I. We are All-American mentions, but more importantly we understood team work and winning. Without an extended essay, Mannie's career and my career at the U of I are comparable to that of Jackie Robinson's making it in major league baseball. Together, we were able to overcome all the road blocks and obstacles of the pre-civil rights era.

It has been a long and good ride during the decades that we have known each other. "Jack" has numerous good qualities, but there's one that stands out more so that the rest. That quality is the drive/desire to succeed and to be "numero uno." I never looked upon that as egotism or extreme vanity. Pride and self respect – that's what comes to mind. You know of his basketball prowess, but when he was on the track team, he wanted to jump higher and run faster than any of his opponents.

Winning was what it was all about. Mannie is my life-long friend and his achievements in the business world and life in general are beyond written description. "Jack" as I call him, always reaches for perfection and more often than not, he achieves excellence.

Govonor Vaughn
Retired Executive, Detroit Edison
Director of Alumni Relations for the Harlem Globetrotters

I first heard of Mannie when he was in the Personnel Department in Boston. We got him transferred back to headquarters in Minneapolis where he went to work under one of our best marketing executives. He was charged with putting together a business plan for a new venture in communications to present to our Management Committee. I personally tore his business plan apart! He went back to the drawing board; presented a new plan which was approved; and that experience gained him even more respect with me and the other members of the Committee. After servicing with distinction in the role of President and General Manager, he rose to become Chief Worldwide Marketing executive under one of my successors, and played an important role nationally in business relations with South Africa.

I was pleased to support Mannie when he decided to buy the Harlem Globetrotters. That he made a great success in reviving the franchise was no surprise to me. What I admire most about Mannie is his great success and his enthusiastic willingness to share his success through philanthropy. He is an outstanding example of those who earn it, should share it with others. I firmly believe in the mantra myself, and salute Mannie for carrying it out.

Edson W. Spencer
Former Honeywell Chairman and CEO

I had the privilege of meeting and getting to know Mannie Jackson at the University of Illinois back in the fall of 1958. Mannie was a star on the Varsity basketball team and I was an incoming freshman ineligible to play on varsity but through practicing with the varsity gained a first-hand appreciation of his skills and talents but more important his character as a human being. In my sophomore year and Mannie's senior year we played together in the back court and developed a real friendship out of mutual respect and in particular our similar humble beginnings.

Mannie's success as a business man was not unexpected because of his ability to focus on goals and seek to be as successful as possible with his incredible work ethic. We share so many interests together with our primary passion centering around the game of basketball. As teammates, as fellow board members with Basketball Hall of Fame it has been a remarkable journey for someone who climbed the ladder in an extraordinary fashion. His philanthropy is unquestioned and his commit-

ment to his causes are unmatched. All coming from someone who started with so little. Our personal journey covers over 50 years and it has been my personal privilege to call him a friend of whom I am very proud.

Jerry Colangelo
President of JHC Partnership
Former Owner/President of Phoenix Suns
Former Owner/President of Arizona Diamondbacks

I first met Mannie Jackson in October of 1956. It was in Huff Gym on the campus of the University of Illinois. I had watched Mannie play for Edwardsville High School in the State Basketball tournament finals on television in March of 1956. His team lost the title game by one point, but he was amazing in defeat and was soon selected the State's number one basketball player.

Mannie was recruited to come to the U of I to play basketball. I was a freshman who wanted to be a manager for the Illinois basketball team.

It was the beginning of four years together with the Fighting Illini. We both were named to Sachem (Activities and Academic Honor Society) – the junior men's honorary at the U of I, and next year to Mawanda (Activities and Academic Honor Society), the senior men's honorary when Mannie was elected captain of our team, and I was senior manager. That Mannie Jackson went on to greatness in life is no surprise to me.

Mannie Jackson was then and throughout his career a leader. Yes, he had great athletic talent when he was captain at Illinois, but he drove himself to excel. Mannie was not a rah-rah type, but a hard worker who led by example.

He was an unselfish player who exemplified teamwork, all qualities that led to his success in the business world after his graduation. Our paths have crossed since those days – most recently when I helped recruit Mannie to serve on the University of Illinois Foundation Board. The University has no better representative for itself than Mannie Jackson, and I am proud to have been involved in the process.

Dennis Swanson
Executive Director NBC Affiliate New York City
Past President ESPN and Wide World of Sports

In the more than 10 years that I was a silent partner of Mannie's in the Harlem Globetrotters, we did not have one acrimonious or disagreeable moment (a rare thing in business these days). I was instrumental as an investor in the acquisition, but Mannie provided the truly inspirational leadership and marketing skills that transformed the Harlem Globetrotters from a marginal organization into a very successful and profitable franchise business. Importantly, he achieved the transformation with a sense of integrity that is rare and was truly remarkable.

It has been my honor and privilege to have been Mannie's friend and business partner for many years. His accomplishments are indeed legendary.

Dennis Mathisen
President, Marshall Group

CONCEIVE

BELIEVE

RECEIVE

ACHIEVE

Dedications

To my wife Cathy, my father Emmett, sister Marjorie (Porge) and children Randall, Cassandra, & Candace; and the dozens of mentors and friends who have helped and taught me along the way. I've been inattentive at times and have made mistakes. I dedicate this story to their support, their forgiveness, their love, and their tolerance.

Special Remembrance:

Dr John Watson, the teammate and friend that put the stepping stones in to usher a fellow ballplayer into corporate life and brave new world. I will always remember the good times with the pioneer.

DREAM PLANNING WORKBOOK

Table of Contents

FIRST QUARTER: CONCEIVE

Chapter 1—Childhood of Courage
Step 1—Launch Your Courage
CONCEPT PRACTICED: Courage to Dream
Three Plays: Fear Check, Fear Reactions, and Top Fears

Chapter 2—Driving Desire to the Hoop
Step 2—Drive Your Desires
CONCEPT PRACTICED: Conscious Belief Systems
Three Plays: Pure Desire, Core Beliefs, and Perfect Day

Chapter 3—Expanding My View
Step 3—Free Your Imagination
CONCEPT PRACTICED: Imagination Stimulation
Three Plays: Bucket List, The Eulogy, and Genie Grants Three

SECOND QUARTER: BELIEVE

Chapter 4—My College Stage
Step 4—Stage Your Dream
CONCEPT PRACTICED: Visualization Expressed
Three Plays: Uniquely You, Visualization Style, and Dream Acting

Chapter 5—Slam Dunking the Globetrotters Dream!
Step 5—Pen Your Dream Script
CONCEPT PRACTICED: Power of Words—Write it!
Three Plays: Dream Decree, Dream Theme, and Dream Elements

Chapter 6—Basketball Dreams to Business Dreams
Step 6—Set Your Dream on Fire
CONCEPT PRACTICED: Ignite Dream Momentum
Three Plays: Self-Energy, Focus on the Ball, and Dream Momentum

THIRD QUARTER: RECEIVE

Chapter 7—Honeywell Dream Well Done
Step 7—Publish Your Dream Plan Book
CONCEPT PRACTICED: Connect with the Thinking Stuff
Three Plays: Title It, Input It, Publish It!

Chapter 8—Harlem Globetrotters Live On!
Step 8—Inspire Your Dream with Action
CONCEPT PRACTICED: Power of the Present Moment
Three Plays: Meditation Action, Now Action, Proactive Action

Chapter 9—That Family Blessing
Step 9—Awaken Your Dream with Thanks
CONCEPT PRACTICED: Attraction Action of Gratitude
Three Plays: Now Thanks, Daily Thanks, Proactive Thanks

FOURTH QUARTER: ACHIEVE

<u>Chapter 10—My Latest Greatest Dream</u>
<u>Step 10—Become a Dream Achiever</u>
CONCEPT PRACTICED: Live, Share, Expand Your Dream
Final Play: Now Dream Big

<u>**EPILOGUE—Mannie's Words of Wisdom**</u>

<u>**DREAM PLAN BOOK TUTORIAL**</u>—Getting Started with Your Dream Plan Book

<u>**DREAMS TO REALITY STEPS**</u> — Ten Dreams To Reality Steps

<u>**DICTIONARY OF TERMS**</u> — Key word definitions

<u>**POWERFUL RESOURCES**</u> — Books, movies, and websites you may access to enhance and further your study and understanding of the ***Dreams to Reality Process***.

<u>**ABOUT THE AUTHORS**</u>— Mannie Jackson & Deborah S. Nelson

CONCEIVE

BELIEVE

RECEIVE

ACHIEVE

Introduction

I am sitting in the company of eleven wealthy CEO's in a recently renovated thirty-second floor mahogany lined boardroom of a 12 billion dollar Fortune 100 company. In this lavish conference room there is over 250 thousand dollars of state of the art electronics at our fingertips. This includes a dozen videophones, a 120-inch Sony Video conference service and 16 speakerphone receivers with 12 language instant translators, and dozens of security devices. Food service for at least 50 completely rotates every 3 hours to keep us supplied with fresh coffee, fruit, or snacks between meals. This is a first-class well-managed company lead by Jim, its 48-year old chairman who cares about its customers, employees, and shareholders as if each entity were the chairman's children.

I literally pinched myself to believe that a child born in a railroad boxcar and raised in dirt-poor poverty in southern Missouri could escape the relentless grip of the poverty cycle and pre-civil rights legal racism to be elected to serve on the board of six of the most powerful and internationally respected fortune 500 companies; each paying between 150,000-450,000 annually, and at the same time owning and managing The Harlem Globetrotters, one of the most well known and enduring brands and companies in the world. The surprising thing to me was that few wanted to believe that an African American and former player could own outright such an iconic brand. After fifteen consecutive years of growth at an average annual rate of 15%, even former players believed I was a front for someone else. The scars of racism and slavery are deeply imbedded in the paychecks of blacks, and too often become the seeds of distrust, fear and skepticism. My dream was to become a competent leader in whatever field I chose and to be a benevolent role model. Board affiliations afforded me the convenience and luxury of moving around the country in a private aircraft (my preference was the Citation for its speed, comfort, and range). And many times I found myself asking out loud, "Am I Dreaming?"

> "Mannie Jackson is one of America's wealthiest and most successful Black men--a businessman, philanthropist, Harlem Globetrotter, social activist. This personal development story is about the journey made by a Dreamer and about his life-long mentors, coaches, and friends who provided the support and encouragement along the way. As this dreamer travels from an abandoned railway boxcar in Southern Missouri, where he was born to become a multi-millionaire and philantropist, there are scores of great stories and references to racism, friendships, basketball heroics, business deals, African-American achievements, giving back, the other side of education, corporate careers, and family values in this book, which all add up to the achievement of the American Dream. Read, watch, and learn, as Mr. Jackson steps up from boxcar dreamer to slam dunk himself into boardroom realities."
>
> — *Mike Rosenbawn*

My thoughts are interrupted and I remember before this trip is over and I return home, there'll be two more board meetings, one with a small failing company in Minneapolis; and later a non-profit board in Springfield, Mass. where I'll chair the Naismith Memorial Basketball Hall of Fame's annual meeting. In recent years sports icons like the Harlem Globetrotters, CM Newton, Larry Bird, Magic Johnson, Stockton, Phil Jackson, The Admiral, Vitale, Earl Lloyd, Vivian Stringer, Meadowlark Lemon, Kareem, Michael Jordan, Riley, Calhoun, Jim Boeheim, Izzo, etc. have been enshrined and permanently cemented in the games' history with this "Boxcar to Boardroom DREAMER" from the little town of Illmo, Missouri front and center. Every one enshrined was a worthy recipient with great stories. My opinion was that 90% of them would easily be captains of industry or politics.

The last fifteen years have gone by so fast with many great experiences that while I did not understand the element of luck involved in my good fortune, the bottom-line of my success has been an absolute commitment to hard work, my family, childhood community of Edwardsville, Illinois, my mentors, positive relationships, and the god-given gift of intuitive selection of good choices.

These choices have come to me in the form of the same kind of blessings that many others receive and often ignore because they had no faith in their journey. More often people will try and copy someone else's plan and not the one that's been uniquely laid out for them. In a recent church service my minister said "if you are confused over personal priorities and choices, close your eyes, sit quietly and just ask the Lord, "What is your plan for me?" The cornerstone of success is in the ability to listen to your DREAMS and follow their guidance. I'm an ordinary and blessed guy from small town who got swept along in many great experiences and opportunities and I enjoyed the ride and tried to be the best I could be.

The lessons from sports taught me to surround myself with good teammates,, prepare for myself as a leader, and practice, practice, and more practice. When I was a kid I was often pushed aside and accused of being a Dreamer and surprisingly to me, in 1994 a national magazine selected me as one of the nations' 25 top corporate strategists. I thought to myself, "The Dreamer" from Illmo, Missouri had arrived. The problem was I still saw myself as that very hungry and unfulfilled Boxcar kid. To this day I am still hungry, because I believe I've not yet completed the journey laid out for me. I now fight the distractions of past success and wealth, which to me is much more of an obstacle than poverty. The loss of humility is a disease.

So as busy as my life has become, I still look for people to help and share my good fortune as I seek solitude and quiet time to understand what's ahead. My life seems to have gained a greater imbalance of questions over answers. For example, why is my journey so different than my childhood friends and relatives like my Uncle Bob White (we were raised in exactly the same environment. Why would I leave the comfort, security and rewards of corporate life? I had achieved the executive position of Senior VP of Worldwide Marketing. Why would I sell 80% ownership interest in a socially satisfying, smooth running "cash cow" venture that has allowed me to share over $25M with charities? The other question is why would I sell the fast growing and socially positive Globetrotters to a private equity firm with no experience, no interest in philanthropy, and no strategic synergy; and the 3rd bidder on a list of 20 others willing to spend over 100 million dollars? There must be a purpose somewhere.

What more can I do for my children Candace and Cassandra and Randall – to assure the positive outcome of "passing the family torch?" I have no debt and need nothing material and to the best of my ability every member of my family and extended family has been made safe and secure, as well as my support for my favorite philanthropic interests. I have reached a point where I am now hearing message that the timing may be perfect to enter a totally new phase.

In other words, what's next and how soon will future dreams show me the way. My wise & spiritual aunt for example, will only say – maybe it's as simple as giving the mind and body rest after forty years in the struggle.

I am certain of one thing--I've learned to use input from many valued sources combined with my best intuition and at a given time the answers to challenging questions (usually through dreams) has always come to me. In one my earliest meetings with friend and co-writer Deborah Nelson, her response was, "Are you surprised?" When successful icons as they've looked bach and objectively analyzed where they came from, what they have achieved, the mistakes made along the way, the many things that worked and failed; most will privately acknowledge that they often ask themselves "Why me?" And what do I uniquely have that others don't? The answer to me seems obvious- we all have our unique journey.

Life is like basketball and golf – you learn to trust without knowing the outcome. The trick is to keep moving forward whether you succeed or fail and simply put all experiences in your data bank; faith takes care of the rest. My high school coach, Joe Lucco would say "Never stop believing." Many successful people are proud of their acquired skill to see

clearly the difference between dreams and fantasy as their data bank becomes more valuable. A few have owned up to using their mental state to achieve desired outcomes in their private lives.

Some believe their mental state alone can actually affect the collective will of others. Las Vegas illusionists claim so in their stage shows; medical leaders, business giants, politicians, and leaders in sports have learned to rely on the skill. In modern times (excluding the medical profession), I characterize football great Jim Brown as a master as well as Michael Jordan, Tiger Woods, Ronald Reagan, Harry Truman, John Wooden, Babe Ruth and Phil Jackson. Who can deny the unique and lasting global impact of JFK, The Dali Lama, Martin Luther King and hundreds more? There are also some not-so-famous who are masters as well, and many you've heard of as charismatic or intuitive leaders.

Some refer to it as the so called "It factor." Throughout this book Deborah Nelson, my co-writer, will help you actually achieve the "it factor" from your very own dreams by managing your life's data bank.

The Homeopathy physician I see once a month to help me avoid the pitfall of unneeded pharmaceuticals, Dr. Ben (Dr. Ben Ta'ati CCH), has been a great help to me and my family. The first half of each visit he always asks me to recount in detail my dreams since my last visit. His notion is that dreams are the indicator of life direction and predictor of one's future health and the state of one's psyche. My personal biography is used here to help engage you in the process and to share my personal story you as a fellow dreamer.

Through years of moving through social, economic and business structures, I've found that Ms. Nelson's "10 Dreams to Reality Steps," covered in this book outlines bold new insights and strategies for understanding one's journey.

My age group represented the first generation of African-Americans in the U.S.A. to vote, to enjoy access to public facilities, routinely use debt as equity to own businesses, aggressively engage in the highest level of bi-partisan politics. Who would have listened to a dream that saw a black person to be elected president of the United States? Back then, who would have believed that black people would routinely achieve high level corporate leadership positions? All this occurred in the 40 + years since dreamers like Jesse, Malcolm, and Martin said, "I am somebody," "That's enough," and "I have a dream." Come take a walk with my Dream to Reality guru Deborah Nelson and I.

Mannie Jackson

Introduction

    Sometimes the richest and most creative moments are ignited in the most unexpected ways. One day while visiting my cousin Cathy, as a Christmas gift, I gave her a copy of my book *Dreams to Reality*, and to my delight, she read it! Later her husband Mannie, happened upon it and also read it. The next time I came through their town, I saw that Mannie's mind was visibly churning, could almost see smoke coming out of his brain. He had an idea. It was for us to collaborate on a book to weave his life story with the 10 Dreams to Reality Steps.

    As I drove back to Santa Barbara, my mind was alive with sparks, vision, and questions of how we could pull this off. Mannie had handed me the precious manuscript of his life story, and later, as I read it I was shaken, shocked, and inspired to experience his journey. I an honored to be entrusted with his life story.

    As I delved into the idea further, I began to realize how brilliant it was. Mannie's "beyond-belief" story had been sitting for 15 years waiting for a moment such as this. The *dreams to reality* concept had been formulating inside of me for decades. I am honored to merge my life lessons with Mannie's biography for a purpose higher than ourselves— to bring the *dreams to reality* concept to those who want to realize dreams at a practical level. Each chapter of Mannie's life corresponds with each of the *Dreams to Reality* Steps. His life is a progression of bringing dreams to reality, and as you read his life story, we hope you are inspired to work through the workbook; and as his astounding life story unfolds; so will yours.

The workbook is a 10-step guide, designed for you to practice and internalize the *dreams to reality* process. It guides you through the process of writing your own story to author and publish your own *Dream Plan Book*.

The average American spends 29 hours a week watching TV; why not devote three to five hours a week to your *own story*, your *own life*—to direct your *own personal dream story*, what can be more exciting than this?

We invite and challenge you to do so! Become the *Author of Your Dreams*.

Deborah S. Nelson

Instructions for The Workbook

The *10-Step Workbook* is designed to serve as your dream planning workbook. However, instead of giving you exercises, we provide *select* plays. The plays are intended for fun learning because seeing dreams come true, is the ultimate fun!

Just as a championship team practices certain plays to position themselves to win, you can practice these *select plays* to position yourself to mine the desires of your heart and write your story and become author of your dreams!

The plays are preparatory and transformational. Their purpose is to wake up courage, desire, imagination, and the genius hiding deep within you. *Trust that they are gently and subtly doing so.*

Even if you do not consider yourself a great writer, you will uncover an abundance of ideas including what and how to write your own personal dream plan!

This Workbook consists of 10 dream steps—each with *select plays,* and divided into the four basic sections: Conceive, Believe, Receive, and Achieve. You may expect each play to take 5–10 minutes, and each of the 10 steps to take 15–30 minutes.

The Conceive section covers Steps 1–3 in *The Workbook*. In this section, you will conceive and write your dream statement.

The Believe section covers Steps 4–6 in *The Workbook*. In this section, you write your dream script for your *Dream Plan Book*.

The Receive section of the workbook covers Steps 7–9 in *The Workbook*. In this section, you collect photos and graphics to illustrate your *Dream Plan Book,* and select a title for your *Dream Plan Book*.

The Achieve section of the workbook covers Step 10 in *The Workbook*. In this section, you will read, feel, meditate, and review your *Dream Plan Book,* and are encouraged and inspired to live, share, and expand your dreams.

O.K. Now let's get started!

CONCEIVE

BELIEVE

RECEIVE

ACHIEVE

Boxcar Dreams Boardroom Reality
Dreams to Reality Workbook

www.BoxcarDreams.com

FIRST QUARTER: CONCEIVE

Chapter 1:
Childhood of Courage

> *Howie tried to convince me I would be foolish to sacrifice the $50 a week I was averaging shining shoes and cleaning tables in exchange for a higher education.*

In name, the town of Illmo, Missouri, no longer exists. Located on the Mississippi River, approximately 130 miles south of St. Louis, it at one time was known as Illmo-Fornfelt, a merging of two innocuous small southern farm communities. But today, all that remains of that identity is the lettering on decaying buildings. The residue has been re-christened Scott City. Later to gain attention as the region that produced conservative icon Rush Limbaugh, Cape Girardeau, Missouri – eight miles to the north – is now the area's definition point.

Illmo was both a river and a railroad town. It was there I was born in a railroad boxcar to Emmett and Margaret White-Jackson. Emmett, a tall, handsome and bright Navy man and Margaret, a dark-skinned beauty, who toiled as a domestic worker for middle-class, white families.

My maternal grandfather, Alonzo "Lonnie" White, was a straw boss on the Cotton Belt Railroad and one of his perks was a railroad boxcar in which to house his family as he traveled up and down the miles of track supervising up to 20 other blacks. It was hard and dangerous work; I'm told he never complained because first and foremost he had a job and he had the ability to make it important work with a noble purpose. I know also that he was an outstanding baseball player and a noted musician.

As I recall, both through memory and conversations with other family members, the boxcar was compartmentalized to house of the entire Jackson-White family. There was one hard wall down the middle with drapes providing partitions. There was a great room serving as both kitchen and adult bedroom. The common toilet was 100 yards away down a dark path. As the family got bigger a second boxcar was added to form a v-shape.

Given the circumstances of those years, our family home was actually quite nice. We also had a little stairway, three or four steps that led from the ground to the boxcar entrance.

At Christmas time, my grandmother would have decorations on both the inside and outside of the boxcars. My grandmother Lois was a great cook and powerful leader – she stood just under five-feet tall and was a very special lady, making certain our makeshift home was always clean and warm. Working non-stop for 12-14 hours a day, caring for a dozen kids, never drew a complaint or curse word. My grandparents were folks who were able to manage their environment and make the best of it at a very high level (when compared to those around them in similar circumstances). They were no doubt high achievers and themselves dreamers.

I recall my grandmother telling me, "Whatever you see as a home for someone – even if others are critical or laughing – that home is their castle and "is a step up for somebody." And so our attitude was even though people were staring at our place in amusement and thinking this was the worst it could get, we felt we were better off than many, and we were very grateful and always proud of what we had.

Events began to intervene with our existence. My father, age 19 went into the Navy and served overseas during World War II. Life went on in our world and like clockwork, the Elmo-area experienced flooding from the Mississippi almost every spring, which complicated both the railway work and housekeeping process.

My paternal grandfather, Sylvester Jackson, despairing of the situation in Illmo, arrived one day and simply picked up the entire household, placed us in a truck and moved us all (14 in total) to Edwardsville, Illinois, a small town of 3200, 15 miles across the river from St. Louis. There we began to experience the rewards and as well as the painful sutures of social integration in its formative years.

A two-story, four room dwelling built by Sylvester felt like a castle and housed all members of the family. Since I was the only boy without a brother, I slept in the same bed with four uncles – three at the head of the bed and me and Uncle Bob across the bottom. The conversations held by those older uncles, Eugene, Lonnie, and Morris were life changing education on work, financial management, travel, politics of war, race relations, and of course women. Those guys would fight, laugh, and tell stories and debate every issue imaginable until the early hours in the morning. Needless to say "Old Bob" and I learned a lot and only complained about our inability to remain awake for the stories. This first Edwardsville

house still stands directly across the street from the then beautiful and stately all-white high school. We watched students cross the campus to that palace as we were on our way to the blacks-only Lincoln School many blocks way across town. There you could see a five-year-old sitting in a classroom next to a teenager. There were very few books and just four teachers.

Several real heroes emerged from that era, and my step-grandmother, Alma Aitch-Jackson and principal C.C. (as in Christopher Columbus) Jones were two of mine. These were teachers who spent quality, out-of-school time with people like myself eager to learn and help bring us up to par with the white students we would (unknown to us) be joining later in junior high and high school classrooms. My friend and social activist Herman Shaw once said, "That neglected old ghetto building was shameful and not much to look at, but a lot of learning and education went on lead by a fe very sweet and dedicated teachers."

My father came away from the military in 1946 with a really bitter attitude towards racism (I had no idea you were allowed to complain. That was like wishing for a Christmas Day to never end), but my Dad also had surprisingly constructive and proactive feelings. He was a skilled, bright person, even though the best he achieved in the segregated Navy was a cook. That is, until they were under attack in the Pacific, then it was all hands on deck to fight the enemy – whether you were trained to do so or not. I saw a bitter young man work hard on 2 and 3 jobs – dream of better times and talk of a future he felt he'd earned and deserved a shot at. His escape to the Navy was to get training (education) and a steady income to provide for his young wife and family.

After the war he became a laborer, a bartender and manager of a gun club in a world where white-collar jobs for blacks, aside from the few doctors and lawyers, tended to be in teaching or preaching. He became politically active and was one of the outspoken pioneers to accelerate the school integration process at a time when many in the white community were hoping that nightmare thought would go away. Fortunately, Brown vs. board of education and State and Federal Revenue funding accelerated the attention paid to the court ordered federal directive. My Dad and others met nightly among themselves and occasionally with a few heroic white sympathizers who today would be called ultra liberal right wing agitators. As a result of those clandestine activities, his credit was shut off and he lost his primary job. The handshake credit arrangements he enjoyed as a compliant colored man was annulled and the "fly-by-night-off-the-books," loan company foreclosed on his home. As a result, my dad moved on to Chicago to find work, while my sister Marjorie and Mom moved from Edwardsville into the slum ridden public housing projects in nearby Madison, Illinois.

My mother retained her job as a domestic in Edwardsville and each day drove us twenty miles to school in that community. At 14 years of age, I began working for a golf professional named Howie Popham at a local country club. Howie was a good man and after two summers of caddying, shining shoes, washing dishes, etc, he tried to convince me I would be foolish to sacrifice the fifty dollars cash a week I was averaging shining shoes, tending bar and cleaning tables in exchange for so-called higher education. I must admit that the celebrity and exhilaration of having a job, money and independence was becoming an increasingly powerful influence in my life. I began actually believing by having a job, all things my family wanted and needed were possible.

Having a job seemed better than playing basketball and made me feel like an adult. Still, I wanted more. All the stuff my Grandfather preached about hard work, being on time, honesty, leadership practice were making sense now. Howie made his case very convincingly to a 14-year old by saying, "You have the dream job. Who do you know in the "colored" community that's doing better?" I thought to myself, "Shit Howie, I'm a good student, an All-State basketball player – is this it???" Little did I realize at the time, with racism, minimal planning, no discipline and unfocused dreams - this in fact could in fact be it! For the first time in my young life I was introduced to "fear." This was now life's greatest call to action. And for me, the fight began – my obsession was a 24/7 battle to never return to a boxcar, to help my family, and to never, never look back at my friend Howard Popham. For this I needed the kind of courage and risk aversion often founded or birthed from fear.

If one were to measure wealth in terms of the need for courage and courage expended, I would have been a wealthy young man by the age of 14. Perhaps it was the courageousness of my father that inspired me to give up the fifty dollar a week job for the dream of higher education. The ability to conceive a better life was also aided by Harlem Globetrotters' founder Abe Saperstein, my high school coach Joe Lucco, my parents, and hundreds of others in the community of Edwardsville. I didn't care about school or understanding the abstract concept of going to school as a means to a better life. Looking back over the landscape of my youth, the decision to risk that fifty dollar a week job for the dream of higher education was a key act of faith and courage setting the stage for the many amazing events to follow. To follow any dream, the very first step we must take is a step of courage. Now, let's go to the most important step, the first one, ***Step 1: Launch your Courage.***

Step 1:
Launch Your Courage

Concept Practiced: *Courage to Dream*

Fear is an illusive giant. What is it? What color is it? How is it shaped? Where can it be found? Fear is everywhere and no where at the same time. It has no shape, color, sound, form or solid visibility. We can see and feel only its effects. What to do when fear is stalking? STOP. TURN AROUND. Look at it square in the face, And what? Fear has no eyes, no face, and no form. The truth is that fear is:

FALSE
EVIDENCE
APPEARING
REAL

This step prepares you to overcome fear, and gather up the courage to write your dream plan and to build your **Dream Plan Book.**

A wise Eddie Rickenbacker once said, "Courage is doing what you're afraid to do. There can be no courage unless you're scared."

This truth brings us straight to the condition of fear. Fear is instinct gone wild! It is a protective mechanism designed to keep us safe in the wild.

What is fear? It's the hidden evil monster under our childhood bed; the unseen wild animal that caused our ancestors to hover in caves to avoid being eaten, and today, it's the dreaded Friday afternoon "pink slip."

Modern day fear has transformed into massive social pressure. If we don't look good, smell good, drive the right car, wear the right clothing, pay our bills exactly on a schedule; we feel and fear our very livelihood is threatened.

When we combine analytical thinking with instinct, the dangerous result can be unrealistic, unhelpful fears, and negative imaginations. In fear we expect the worst; imagine something bad that happened before, or imagine our survival threatened while perfectly safe. By focusing on fear we create a self-fulfilling prophecy. Untreated fear can cause procrastination, indecision, blaming, immobilization, insecurity, and excuses, which all slow the realization of our dreams. *Faith neutralizes fear. Instantly. When we act in fear, our nightmares come true. When we act in faith, we see our dreams come to life.*

PLAY 1-1: Fear Check

Concept Practiced: *Courage to Dream*

PLAY 1-1: Write the numbers 1 through 5 next to the fears listed below; with 1 being the weakest intensity to 5 being the strongest intensity—0 if not a common fear for you. Then draw a circle around your three most intense fears!

> **SAMPLE PLAY 1-1**
>
> *Underlying fears that I have been suppressing— fear of poverty, fear of people, fear of the world, and fear of authority are my most intense fears.*

☐ Fear of the Unknown

☐ Fear of Failure

☐ Fear of Success

☐ Fear of Dying

☐ Fear of Flying

☐ Fear of Abandonment

☐ Fear of the World

☐ Fear of People

☐ Fear of Intimacy

☐ Fear of Poverty

☐ Fear of Illness

☐ Fear of Change

☐ Fear of Disapproval

☐ Fear of Authority

☐ Other_____

☐ Other_____

☐ Other_____

☐ Other_____

☐ Other_____

☐ Other_____

☐ Other_____

PLAY 1-2: Fear Reactions

Concept Practiced: *Courage to Dream*

PLAY 1-2: Check off the reactions your fears cause and list the fear associated with it next to it:

> **SAMPLE PLAY 1-2**
>
> *My reaction to the fear of answering the phone is creating habitual procrastination in my career and preventing me from reaching my full potential and seeing my dreams come to reality.*

Check off appropriate boxes then fill in the blanks to the right of the reaction enter the associated fears that tends to cause that reaction

☐ Procrastination_____

☐ Indecision_____

☐ Immobilization_____

☐ Insecurity_____

☐ Excuses_____

☐ Blaming_____

- ☐ Irresponsibility_____
- ☐ Sleeplessness_____
- ☐ Overeating_____
- ☐ Under eating_____
- ☐ Avoidance_____
- ☐ Anti-Social_____
- ☐ Other_____
- ☐ Other_____
- ☐ Other_____
- ☐ Other_____
- ☐ Other_____
- ☐ Other_____
- ☐ Other_____
- ☐ Other_____

PLAY 1-3: Top Fears

Concept Practiced: *Courage to Dream*

PLAY 1-3: Choose your top fears (in order of intensity); and write down what reaction these fears typically cause in you.

> **SAMPLE PLAY 1-3**
>
> *I am aware of my fear of flying, speaking, and death. I will replace these fears with newer, happier affirmations and beliefs, the moment I become aware that these fears are clouding my focus.*

1. _____

2. _____

3. _____

Release Fear to Launch Your Courage

Concept Practiced: *Courage to Dream*

Winston Churchill once said, "There is nothing to fear but fear itself."

And that was such a profound statement, because the object of our fear is not what harms us the most. What harms us the most is our fearful reaction. We have only to shine a flashlight under the bed, to make the invisible fear monster disappear.

We can neutralize fear most effectively by cultivating awareness of "pet fears" to move through them. Shine the light…talk about them, write about them, and take note of them during the day when they pop up in thoughts. Instead of pushing them away, begin to substitute with words of faith. The more they hide, the bigger they get! Feel the fear; shine your light of your awareness and faith on them to release your hold on fear, and fear's hold on you. There's nothing like taking fear and transforming it into powerful action! It takes practice to make transforming fear to courage a new habit. Step into the new "promised land" of faith and personal success.

SAMPLE CONCLUSION

Fears create limitations and becoming aware of them allows me to release them. Unless I am in immediate physical danger, these fears are simply built-in protective instincts that do not apply to most situations; and misapplied fears are detrimental to my growth.

Now that you have practiced these plays, make an inspirational comment to yourself about overcoming fears and using that power to launch your courage to dream!

Chapter 2:

Driving Desire to the Hoop

> *I became single-minded about improving my game, which I did by practicing every night and day, rain or shine and my mother threatened to have me committed if I didn't stop dribbling the "damn" ball.*

As a 10-12 year-old, I wasn't the greatest athlete. I just wasn't focused on games- too much scary stuff going on in my household – like finding food, getting wood and coal for the stove and finding some space. I was tall, frail, and a little clumsy. The first sports team I tried out for, I didn't make the final roster. I was that kid who often got ridiculed because I wanted to be with the best players and would stand at the back of the group when they were choosing sides during recess. And then I would overhear someone saying, "I don't want that dude," and Jessie Browne would say, "Don't put him in this game."

I also remember a basketball game played in East Louis. Lincoln School was getting beaten badly. With 10 seconds to go, Coach Woods called me in with the score 66 to 15. Little did I know that some older East Louis guys had bet against our little team scoring more than 15 points. As luck would have it the ball came to me and I shot quickly and scored. The place went crazy. I assumed everyone was cheering for me and then a fight broke out. We left in a real hurry and once inside our little school bus, they tried to turn it over before we could drive off.

We were scared and shaking until we got couple miles down the road...at which time our coach looked at me and yelled "Shooter, why the heck did you of all people shoot the ball?" Everyone broke out laughing! I laughed, but at that moment I didn't understand the joke and I really hated Basketball. When my athletic accomplishments became media events, most of my childhood friends were somewhat shocked, but many were not surprised. They knew about my work habits, desire, and commitment and after all I was said and done, "The Shooter."

My world began to change the first time I heard the "Brother Bones" rendition of the song Sweet Georgia Brown and at age 12 when I first saw the Harlem Globetrotters. The reaction of the crowds and the things the Globetrotter players would do on the basketball court truly amazed me. I remember walking up to Abe Saperstein, who founded the team in Chicago, Illinois, and told him that someday I was going to play for him. He shook my hand and said he would look forward to that day after I finished college. I remember thinking, "What the heck does college have to do with it?" I'm sure he told a million little kids like me the same thing. But for me it stuck.

The Globetrotters slick routines and style and that song Sweet Georgia Brown played over and over in my mind. One day while working at LeClaire Park in Edwardsville, Illinois, sweeping off the basketball courts, I discovered that I could jump higher and run faster than everyone my age. I quickly learned to hang on the basketball rim and actually dunked a tennis ball and later that summer a basketball. I was only 12 at the time and 5'10" tall, so the skill got noticed. When the Globetrotter movie GO MAN GO and HARLEM GLOBETROTTERS' STORY came out, I camped out in the Wildy Theater. I saw it at least 10 times and began to dream the story, the only difference was, the movie had me in it. I was William "Bill" Townsend (Rookie Brown) and Marques Haynes combined. Needless to say, my self-image skyrocketed in those 2 hours, I saw my role models and dream. When my school integrated, I was one of three black kids (the quota system) selected by Coach Gregor to join the junior high team.

Very quickly, I went from a substitute, who could jump to leading scorer after discovering the magic of practice and repetition, I also could shoot the basketball in this weird looking Globetrotters manner. I quickly realized I had something and became single minded about improving my game, which I did by practicing every night and every single day, rain or shine. My mother threatened to have me committed if I did not stop dribbling the "damn" ball. It was at this time I began to set goals, and seriously dreamed of being special and of going to college so that I could eventually do the Globetrotter thing. And I'd ask, "what would it take" to anyone who would listen.

The other 3 blacks on that historical high school team were my lifelong best friend Govoner Vaughn, Jim Vaughn, and my younger uncle, Bob White. Our white teammates included Jim Chandler, Rich Pulliam, Lee May, and Gordon Mallory. Kenneth "Buzz" Shaw, who retired as President of Syracuse University, and Harold Patton, an internationally recognized and leading patent attorney for Medtronic Corporation in Minneapolis. Four of the starting five became division one players, college grads, and have remained friends to this day. Govoner and I also enjoyed professional basketball careers. I often say – I cannot imagine achieving what I have without his friendship. My buddy Gov was "the real deal." We were each other's biggest fan and even though we didn't care that much or know why we breezed through college together. were so close, his mother seemed to treat us equally and actually maintained my scrapbook, which I cherish to this day. together.

As eighth graders, we never lost and were the talk of the state. Including my Uncle Bob, the same group formed the nucleus of the High School varsity team under the watchful eye of a smart and tough Italian teacher/coach named Joe Lucco. Coach Lucco would eventually become the single most unforgettable inspiration in my life. He was a leader, and excellent teacher of the game, and if race was ever a problem for him, he disguised it well. Coach never gave me any slack, but I knew he cared deeply for me. He would always say he demanded more from me because he knew I had more to give. I never really understood what he was saying until much later. All I know is that he made me feel as if anything was possible and gave me the driving desire to be the best at whatever I choose to do. For examples, he knew that Bob White (Uncle Bob) and I would stay in the gym two hours after every home game to practice and replay every shot – he also knew that the night janitor paid us a dollar and trusted us to turn out the lights and clean the locker room. Lucco understood our dreams and supported them. When an important exam came up he called me to say "this was important, bring us an A or B+, we can do it. Little did I know he had a side bet with the teacher that I'd get an A or B.

We had many challenges other than outscoring an opponent during those years. On road trips, we couldn't eat in most restaurants with our white teammates. This was true even in our hometown. Imagine a player averaging nearly 30 points a game, being Mr. Basketball of the State, eating in a kitchen across the street from his high school while all the fans, media, students, and white teammates looked on from the dining room. During the tournaments in Southern Illinois that involved overnight stays, we were offered lodging with families of color because hotels wouldn't always accept us. Even own team towels were dyed black and orange – one stack for myself, Gov, Bob and Jim Vaughn, and one for our white teammates. Coach Lucco would say focus on the big stuff; one day you will own this town and they'll name this school after you. Let's you and me get there together, and he'd say in a kind and sly way" by the way "shooter" take any towel you want this is your team. With his help, I learned the importance of focussing on the right things and eventually we made black towels an important symbol of our strength not our weakness and everybody wanted them.

Basketball was a lot like my experiences in business--I kept tinkering with it and it came natural to me.

We heard all the racial epithets shouted from the crowds – nigger, jungle bunny, etc. Of course we were fully prepared to fight but we didn't; because we loved our coaches and teammates and didn't want to jeopardize our growing stature as a team. Most often Gov and I would calmly go about the business of winning games and embarrassing opponents.

Through the guidance of Lucco we quickly learned that the most powerful weapon in our arsenal was our talent and we'd set out to embarrass all opponents without showing emotion. We would often hear booing and obscene language turn to applauds and words of praise. Because of Gov I learned to appreciate successes without letting it destroy our future, little white kids would wait for us after games just to touch us. Media from all over the country photographed our every move. Only the most beautiful young girls from the opposing team schools, black and white, had nerve to approach us. We would look at each other, then Lucco, and quietly move on laughing. Later we'd laugh out loud and recount hundreds of stories and experiences. We felt we had the world and sports community by the short hairs. It was fun. We still get together to this day and fuss and laugh over those memories.

Gov and I always had our own little games going on within a game; where we would strive to get far enough ahead and to give the audience something to remember and talk about. One of our favorite sayings was, "Let's meet upstairs or uptop," which meant we intimidated by jumping as high as possible over the rim. A gentleman named Spike Riley would give me a half-dollar if I dunked the first score of the game. Gov at 6'4," would easily claim the tip and let me chase it down for the dunk. Coach Joe Lucco loved it! We also heard about complaints from white parents about our taking their kid's roster spots and playing time away from the "regular (white) kids." Because of Lucco and the quality of the guys in our group, we never had a single incident within the team.

Even in Southern Illinois, where an unlikely recently integrated small school was creating an athletic fable, acceptance off the playing field had its limits. A former Chicago Bear and National Football League all-star, was county sheriff and father of Toni, one of our best friends and the team's most popular cheerleaders.

The sheriff owned the largest and most popular downtown restaurant where I at one time shined shoes and where everyone went to celebrate following an out-of-town victory. The

Maybe that's why I'm a little weird today because I truly care about everyone. In the business had a strict no-blacks served policy no matter what the circumstances. It amazed me then and still does today that many white people only believe blacks are special and good folk when they aren't complaining about stupid and insensitive conditions and values. It makes me sick even today to recount the hypocrisy of those times by seemingly good people. I wanted to know about everyone and I would meticulously maintain sensitivity profiles and individual scouting reports.

I owe my judgment to my Dad and Grandfather who saw a bigger picture for me and encouraged Coach Lucco to keep the pressure on. I was also lucky to have a talented, smart, good-humored sidekick in teammates Bill Pendleton and Gov Vaughn.

So after a night when Govoner and I had led the team to a win, we joined our relatives who were working in the kitchen and had a great meal, complements of the employees. I remember looking through the small opening where they served the food and seeing our teammates, their girlfriends and families. Some might come up and say, "Nice game Mannie, Gov," and we would speak to them through that small hole in the wall. We weren't allowed to join them and to my knowledge no one thought that to be hypocritical or ignorant. I remembered Lucco message and thought one day maybe I will own this "joint."

It was a positive time for Govoner and me because we were proud and dominant players who commanded respect and received a large degree of adulation throughout the Midwest. We definitely weren't hoodlums; we were good country kids and good students (Personally I cared nothing about school and education. I had to do it to paly ball and sitting by came easy.) who developed lasting friendships with almost everyone – especially our teammates. Still, I don't recall one teammate or administrator ever saying he felt badly when we were turned away at a hotel or restaurant. It was just accepted as the way of life at that time. I dreamed for the day that I could write the rules. My Dad would say, "He who has the gold, writes the rules."

Gov and I would dream about better times and I'd frequently vent my frustration at the system while gaining a reputation of someone not to push too far. And I always knew that Gov "had my back" and that hundreds of others, black and white, supported us unconditionally. An older family friend, Wes McMurray once said "Gov and I had become unknowingly the fulfillment and inspiration for the dreams of many of his generation." I then understood why Old Wes sent $3-5 dollars to me regularly as encouragement to get an education and stay out of trouble.

Our last two years at Edwardsville, we advanced to the quarterfinals and finals of the Sweet 16, Illinois' state high school tournament. This included all schools in the state as Illinois was not broken down by classification, even though our little school had less than 800 students and the town population was 5800 and less than 250 blacks (five in my graduation class). I scored just under 30 points per game and was selected All-State as a junior and senior year and Illinois Player-of-the-Year as a senior.

At 6'2" I had a 44-inch vertical leap and enjoyed bounding over people and dunking. Old Gov, who was 6'4", (happens to be the greatest clutch shooter I've ever seen), and I had fun and tried to share it with everyone. There was no place we wouldn't go to take on a challenge. And black folks from everywhere would bet hundreds of dollars on our reputation and performance during summer play. We were never fazed by it; we'd lifted 40-80 pound brick racks 8 hours a day at Richard's brickyard and chased the next big pick-up game every night. Late into the night we would sit around and replay those games as we ate eat Barbecue ribs, catfish, and drank orange soda water while listening to the Dells, Sam Cooke, The Chantels. B B King, Ike and Tina Turner, and the best blues artists in the country.

I dreamed endlessly of being the best and reaching the top; but no one bothered to caution me about the road blocks and the scale of the impersonal reality of racism. Or maybe I was just too drugged by success and sports adoration that I didn't listen closely enough. Basketball and my hometown comfort very likely blinded me temporarily and certainly we had no frame of reference since racism and segregations was all we knew. Basketball and life in a small midwest down was all we knew. There was no TV, no CNN or YouTube. All dreams, strategies, and aspirations should factor in obstacles and barriers and with the right preparation, winning is still very possible. My own story would serve as exhibit A.

As an example of how detached my family became to all the sports stuff, my mother attended one or two games, my grandfather Jackson came to one game and left at halftime; we had stopped playing so he assumed the noisy game was over. He was a great believer of hard work, setting goals and striving to achieve them. He never understood the concept of using all that youthful energy to play a game. He'd say to me it's alright to do sports if you don't let it get in the way of important things. Up until his death he was in disbelief that schools would give all expense paid scholarships to student athletes and that one would aspire to actually make a living playing a game. He would really be shocked to know that in 2010 the sports industry was larger in revenue than the entire auto industry – and that millionaire athletes are made every day in sports. I am not sure I want to believe it either. Imagine twenty plus years at Honeywell and in just ten years with the Globetrotters, I had accumulated 20 times more personal equity and wealth plus a lifetime of memories and goodwill. Grandfather, Mother, Father, Howie Popham, and Coach Lucco would never understand that math.

All four would have also been proud to watch me give the 2009 University of Illinois commencement speech and meet my friend and then President of the university, Joe White. Joe is a brilliant person who lives his life in perfect balance. Whenever I met and talked with his wife, it becomes my personal revival.

Joe Lucco was in great demand as a post-season banquet speaker and took me along for the 2-3 hour drives and we'd talk for hours about things in life other than basketball. He is the person who taught me how to knot a necktie. He would sometimes look over at his son Billy (now a prominent attorney) and tell audiences that I was like another son to him.

One almost could see racial attitudes shifting on those evenings. He was a powerful and excellent speaker who inspired audiences with his stories, value system, and accomplishments – not the least of which was his competitive advantage of being able to motivate and develop the black student-athlete. He would conclude his talks by saying I'm good at what I do because I love what I do and I've learned to chase my dreams and BELIEVE – after a pause following a standing ovation he would look over at me and simply say in a muted tone not always heard by everyone "not bad for a first generation Italian." We'd exit the building like rock stars and start the drive home. He later became superintendent of Schools and concluded his career as an Illinois State Senator.

For all his flamboyance and success, Lucco took a genuine interest in Govoner and me academically. Our first seven years in black-only schools left us woefully under prepared for the curriculum we'd be expected to master in integrated classrooms. As an example, I'd never had an English class where prepositions and nouns were discussed. Talk about embarrassing! The white students would snicker so loud that class would be suspended and teachers would admonish their behavior(that was also embarrassing) I was slowly learning to dislike school.

Two teachers, Ms. Moomaw and Ms. Edwards, apparently saw something in us and became mentors. They took me into their homes and their hearts, and spent hours bringing me up to speed in math, reading, English and other courses essential to catching up. One of them gave me my first book at age 12, SNOWBOUND by John Greenleaf Whittier. Of all the educators I encountered, they most of all helped make the reality of college possible.

How critical was their help? Govoner and I went to one of the country's largest and most respected schools – the University of Illinois. On the admission test, which I didn't expect to do well, I scored in the upper 20% in English and Science. My Uncle Bob on the other hand was very smart, with superior basketball talents, but could not get on top of things academically. He and Bill Penelton, also smart, were all-star level players, but to this day, I blame educational apartheid for damaging their development and wasting their talents. Aside from being solid people and superior athletes, both could well have become top lawyers, physicians or educators if it were not for our country's separate and so-called equal school situation. Their lives were severely disrupted through no fault of their own. They were and are gifted individuals whom I respect and love immensely. My story is designed to provide a "lighthouse" or "beacon of hope" for people on the edge of losing hope.

One of the most under-stressed stories of that era are the people who couldn't compensate for the academic distance lost before integration. My friend Sam was a wonderful athlete, but he could not adjust to all the social change. He never felt legitimate or confident anywhere but on the playing field. He spent several years in mental institutions and I believe buckled under the pressure of racism. attempting to catch up and be accepted in a world he had never known. He later spent several years in mental institutions and I believe buckled under the pressures of racism. He became just one of many tragic stories of those times.

Keeping Sam in mind…don't you let others with their limited beliefs in you take you down and steal your dreams and desires. Remember, do not be influenced by haters and do not validate their existence by being influenced by them. So next we will playfully dive into *Step 2-Drive Your Desires*, to identify and intensify your pure passions and desires to drive your dream to reality. Let's go to with Deborah to *Step 2* right now!

Step 2:

Drive Your Desires

Concept Practiced: *Conscious Belief Systems*

Consciously scan the UNCONSCIOUS beliefs that no longer server your highest purpose. Consciously and continuously replace them with your truest, deepest desires, passions, and purpose. These God-given desires will drive your dreams!

Do you drive your desires? Or do unconscious beliefs drive you?

The purpose of this step is to bring your truest desires to the surface of your imagination; to spark up your own true dreams, and to discard dreams you have allowed others to impose upon you.

You will learn, through these plays, to apply your true desires to change unconscious belief systems that drive you to serve others' visions. You will direct your honest and pure desires into conscious belief systems to serve your visions and dreams.

What is desire? It is the power of pure passion. We are trained to believe that our desires are wrong; that they will betray us. Yet our truest desires actually fuel personal power seeking to be manifested. If we want to be powerful enough to realize our dreams, we will acknowledge our desires as a natural expression of who we are. To deny our desires is to deny the truth within ourselves.

Our deepest, truest desires are given us by our Creator, with intent to inspire something unique and significant in you. The following plays are designed to help you to bring out your truest desires so that you may to begin to conceive your dream.

Belief Systems

As children, we are raised with traditional belief systems, which we automatically and subconsciously have applied to adulthood. However, if we are to get beyond survival, to live our dreams, we must inevitably examine the belief systems passed down that have taught us to play it safe—trading safety and comfort for the passions of life.

All of our lives most of us have been unconsciously accepting and living by belief systems implanted in us by "powers that be." We will examine these belief systems to see how and if they serve our highest potential or if they serve the highest potentials of others.

PLAY 2-1: Pure Desire

Concept Practiced: *Conscious Belief Systems*

PLAY 2-1: Imagine yourself as a young child once again. Make a list of gifts you want for Christmas. If you do not celebrate Christmas, make a list of gifts you want for your birthday. Or list gifts you would want now.

> **SAMPLE PLAY 2-1**
>
> *The theme of most of the gifts that I want is the prevalent desire to be in and around beauty, and beautiful places.*

1. _____
2. _____
3. _____
4. _____
5. _____

PLAY 2-1: What is the commonality in the things that you desire? What is the predominate theme? Where is the heart of your desires?

PLAY 2-2: Core Beliefs

Concept Practiced: *Conscious Belief Systems*

PLAY 2-2: Check off these core beliefs you have held that no longer serve you.

> **SAMPLE PLAY 2-2**
>
> *I resolve to replace the core belief that I am not good enough with the empowering belief that says I approve of myself! Every time I hear my inner self say that I am not good enough, I will replace the thought with "I wholeheartedly and enthusiastically approve of myself!"*

Check to the left of the items if this is a core belief for you. Continued on next page.

- [ ] There is not enough
- [ ] I am not good enough
- [ ] I am not pretty or handsome enough
- [ ] I am not young enough
- [ ] I am not smart enough
- [ ] I am not rich enough
- [ ] I am not giving enough

Check off these core beliefs that will serve you to achieve your best self

- ☐ I accept and love myself as I am
- ☐ I am becoming the best version of myself
- ☐ I am whole, healed, and perfect
- ☐ I love my life
- ☐ There is always enough
- ☐ All my needs are met
- ☐ There is no failure, only adjustment
- ☐ I completely and wholeheartedly approve of myself
- ☐ I enjoy and respect myself

PLAY 2-2: Practice daily substituting unconscious and worn out beliefs with self-empowering thoughts and feelings! *Write down your new thoughts, and feelings and beliefs here*

1 _____

2 _____

3 _____

4 _____

5 _____

6 _____

7 _____

8 _____

9 _____

10 _____

PLAY 2-3: Perfect Day

Concept Practiced: *Conscious Belief Systems*

PLAY 2-3: Your ideal day consists of the following components:

> **SAMPLE PLAY 2-3**
>
> *When I wake up in my ideal home, I hear the birds singing, and feel the sun shining into my windows. I spend some time in prayer, in meditation, have a cup of latte, and go to the gym in my basement and work out. Then I go to work writing in my home office for 6 hours. At the end of the day, I walk along my private beach as watch the sun set down the ocean's horizon for the end of another incredible, beautiful day.*

1 _____

2 _____

3 _____

4 _____

5 _____

6 _____

7 _____

8 _____

9 _____

10 _____

> **SAMPLE CONCLUSION**
>
> *My inner desires are natural and normal and are meant to drive me to my life's purpose!*

Personal Conclusions about Driving Your Desires _____

_____
_____
_____
_____
_____
_____
_____
_____
_____
_____
_____
_____
_____
_____
_____

Chapter 3:
Expanding The View

> Once in South Africa, the initial impact on Candace was similar to what mine had been. She looked out of a 20th floor hotel window to see the beauty of Johannesburg's skyline. We went to a Sun City resort, attended a play, ate at a finer restaurant, visited a game reserve and walked the beaches of Capetown and Durban.

Like many African Americans back in the day, my first images of Africa were drawn from Tarzan movies. I thought the Dark Continent to be just that – a land of jungle, diseases, wild animals, and European oppressors, who were by the way, caring righteous peoples, and the natives were primitive troublemakers.

I wasn't just ashamed of my African ancestry – at one point in my life, I thought it a joke and actually felt burdened by my association with it. I knew I was not alone in these feelings as I tried to get my Executive Leadership Council membership to stand-up and publicly fight for a Democratic South Africa. Only a few wanted to 'risk' their newly acquired economic status on such an association. However, those that did were simply amazing. Eleanor Williams, Jim Kaiser, Al Martins, Buddy James, Hazel O'Leary, Jackie Robinson, Earl Graves, and Ann Fudge to name just a few.

Obviously, the image changed for me long before 1991 when I visited South Africa to explore future business possibilities for Honeywell Corporation. Still, much of my initial feel for the country had been in the abstract. Black lleaders from Xerox, honeywell, Coca-Cola, Pepsi, and Apple Computers already in the country a were making a difference. Most of all, I loved the fact that Earl Graves who had his own successful publishing business, Black Enterprise, and was always fully engaged in South African business and social issues.

One visit was enough to put a face on the country, the people and the problem. We were stunned to see the similarities of apartheid to our past in the USA and we knew better things were in their future. We realized how far we had come and how much was needed to level the playing field in So Africa. Affirmative action wasn't enough – the gap was simply too great. It was also clear that democracy would be "mess" and a long tedious venture. But most importantly the struggle could be sustained by hope, and a simple belief in the future.

Two things shocked me: first was the incredible beauty of the country. Visually, it is one of had done to another to kill their dreams. I walked through a corporate headquarters as sophisticated as any you ever see in the United States and observed that the wealth of ruling cartels was enormous. In one office, the art on the walls alone was worth a fortune. Despite widespread poverty, only a little research was required to learn there was more than enough land, food, water, and natural resources for everyone to have an adequate share. I remember one of Mandala's aids saying, "Tell your American Friends that we are committed to Democracy, but a democracy based on marality not greed and one where winners do not take all and our brothers and sisters are not left on the side of the road."

Later we drove into a black township, saw the shacks that passed for homes, and met many people. The conditions made our worst ghettos in the United States appear princely by comparison. Hovels that measured 12-by-12 feet and smaller, sheltered as many as a dozen people. Furniture would be something from old hotels, or something even the poorest whites had thrown away. Heat from stoves using coal, gave off environmentally distinctive and deadly fumes and set the eyes to burn. Leaving those homes in the evening, I'd walk bent-over to avoid a layer of smoke that formed a low-level umbrella over the villages of Alexander and Soweto.

I found myself thinking that the bombing of Hiroshima or the devastation in Korea and Vietnam could not have been any more destructive than the apartheid affecting these innocent and sensitive people in their homeland.

Perhaps the most troubling reaction to me of all was personal. The longer I stared at this situation, the larger my eyes grew. Inwardly, I realized that some of what I was witnessing seemed familiar. There were analogies everywhere. Too much of it looked and felt like my past life and my country. So much reminded me of Illmo, Missouri, East St. Louis, Gary, Indiana and hundreds of educationally deprived, racially divided and poverty-stricken townships and communities across America. I remembered feeling and saying at the University of Illinois that "Education is not the problem no will it alone be the solution." What we lacked is a moral common ground. we spend too much time seeding and cultivating our differences.

As a business person, I quickly understood the economics behind what happened here and why all this had to change. The white cartel leaders had to know if they did not initiate a new order in which all people could participate, a violent new order would be forced upon them with a collapse of social order and soon thereafter the South African Economy. In my opinion, the process of dismantling apartheid was not just a moral imperative, but also an economic survival decision for the strongest region in sub-Saharan Africa.

As Nelson Mandela emerged from prison and became the leading force behind the new political order, many American-based companies like Honeywell, Xerox, Sara Lee, Coke, Corning, and Apple – which had divested themselves of South African interests – began consulting with the African National Congress (ANC) about timetables for returning to the country. The American corporate sanctions brought many leading black executives to the forefront and into USA's corporate boardrooms. I came to know Mandela, spent quality time with him and became an advocate for the ANC in the U.S. Most of us were able to persuade our companies not to reinvest until signaled by the ANC and free elections had been mandated.

Honeywell has since had two start-ups in the region. During August of 1994, my then 14-year old daughter, Candace, accompanied me on one of my many South African journeys. Honeywell divested its majority interest in Martech Control and I became its Chairman of its transition and investment interest. It was a pressure packed experience that I cherished. Fortunately, Honeywell's' resident senior manager was an excellent executive and very highly respected by all levels of South African employees.

My daughter Candace had been raised in a comfortable and integrated atmosphere in Minneapolis. When I'd tell either of my daughters how it was in Harlem, South Central L.A., Gary Indiana or Southern Illinois during the 1950's and 60's about racism, poor schools, no rights vote, no use of public toilets, the inability to eat in segregated restaurants, these 50's and 60's stories were as abstract to them as mid-nineties conditions in South Africa seemed to me. The first time Candace and my younger daughter, Cassandra, saw an area where I once lived on the near south side of Chicago, their reaction was a blunt "This place looks awful! Why didn't you just move?"

Candace's previous impressions of South Africa had been television clips of fighting, terror and constant chaos. Before we left home, she wanted to know if we needed guards, or would I have to carry a gun.

Once in South Africa, the initial impact on Candace was similar to what mine had been. She looked out of a hotel window to see the beauty of Johannesburg's skyline. We went to a

Sun City resort, attended a play, ate at a four-star restaurant, visited a game reserve and walked the beaches of beautiful Capetown and Durban. "This is a neat place," she commented. "It must be nice to be wealthy and white here," she added. And added innocently, why are these people so greedy and selfish?

During our visit we drove to Soweto, where Mandela lived before being imprisoned. Some 20 minutes from Johannesburg on a dirt street, on the way we passed the beautiful suburban white district, later the Colored District, and eventually Soweto. What a shock! I was negotiating in the home of a white contractor who was interested in doing more business with Martech; Candace, in another room, struck up a friendship with his daughter.

During an ensuing conversation, I pointed out to Candace that had we lived in South Africa, I could not have worked for a corporation like Honeywell as a business unit president; and that she and her new friend could not have lived in the same housing area. Candace greeted this reality first with disbelief and later with indignation. Saying they have no right to do that. I again thought of my Dad's saying, which was "he who has the gold makes the rules." I then heard myself saying "this will all change one day," because of technological advancements in communications with the outside world and the growing numbers of righteous people both black and white dreaming of a new order and a new reality for this country. I told her that one of these dreamers and leaders is a friend of mine and your mother's, and a he's a smart strong black leader who cares about all people and we'll meet him at the first parliament meeting of the newly elected ANC in a couple days. His public name is Nelson Mandela but as our friend, you will call him Madiba (father).

The dinner after the Parliament session was a massive celebration. We sat around this very large mahogany table next to Lin de Way Mabooza, a charming chief of staff and later his ambassador to Germany. We ate, shared joyful stories, toasted everyone, and we celebrated. Soon thereafter at about midnight, I learned that one the Tribal Chiefs desired my daughters hand in marriage. I was amused, then shocked as I realized this was serious. I immediately excused us and took Candace by the hand and began the 2-mile walk back to our hotel. We were laughing and screaming various version of the story all the way back. About 3 a.m. I was exhausted when I laid my head on the pillow and thought, *what a day and what an experience*. My daughter was safe, happy, and seemingly oblivious to all the possibilities that a father would worry about.

Next day we visited a start-up squatter camp where people lived in conditions unimaginable to Candace, and myself I reminded Candy those conditions may have been forced upon us too, had we been native to this country. Candace met the people and saw that no matter how disadvantaged they were, they greeted one another, laughing, playing, and working together as families and community. She discovered that their most valued asset was like hers—because they too dreamed for a better tomorrow.

I still have a photo of Candace with her arms around two little girls from that camp. She remembers them as bright, inquisitive, and wanting to be friends and to play with an African sister who just happened to live thousands of miles away in another world and in another reality. I couldn't help but wonder about their dreams and what they would later remember about Candace. Looking at Cassandra and Candace always reminds me of how fortunate my life as a person of African decent in the USA has been; and how many other Africans, Asians, Europeans, Hispanics and Indians must feel the same way. In this country we are actually encouraged to live and work side by side and to dream positively and big. That's what I have come to know about my imperfect America.

Cassie and Candy had gone to NYU and both aspired to graduate degrees. Their dreams were to contribute, to lead, and to eventually improve public policy. Both girls are blessed with intelligence and fertile imaginations and the will to go after their dreams. Candace has been a writer reporter for the Wall Street Journal for 5 years after getting a Masters in Journalism from Columbia University while Cassandra finished her education at DePaul. Cassie is our volatile and outspoken revolutionary. As an entrepreneur she's a committed vegan and will one day change the world for the better. My son Randall is my buddy and I've never met anyone with such pure intentions. I regret not supporting and pushing him more. He is creative and passionate about everything he attempts, as an actor he has real talent with a great sense of humor. Randall is one of the easiest people to be around for 15 minutes or 15 days. He is always completely in the moment.

Speaking of kids, I remember looking into the eyes of those South African children and seeing myself in Illmo, Missouri at that same age. My grandmother was right, the Illmo boxcar where I was born would have been a giant step up for these people! Being in that far away land changed my perspective and also aroused my anger.

Having navigated my way out of my own apartheid American township, (which my dad refers to affectionately as THE VILLAGE), and reflecting on the South African Ghetto townships reminded me of how key imagination is in bringing our dreams to reality. To imagine a different life, a better life, a new dream is necessary before stepping into it. It's also near impossible to imagine what you've never seen without faith and help from teachers, mentors, or coaches. And now, in the digital era there's a new excuse for denying imagination and dreams while neglecting to define life strategies. This next step takes an active, stimulated imagination. Now let's go to Step 3 to begin to learn how to expand and to practice freeing your imagination!

Step 3:
Free Your Imagination

Concept Practiced: *Imagination Stimulation*

"*There is a thinking stuff from which all things are made, and which, in its original state, permeates, penetrates, and fills the interspaces of the universe. A thought in this substance produces the thing that is imaged by the thought*"

—*Wallace D. Wattles*

The purpose of this step is to stimulate and expand your imagination. In preparation for writing your **Dream Plan Book,** you will identify your desires and dreams! Once you identify your desires, you will get clues about your true passion and purpose, and your most heartfelt dreams will awaken something unique and significant in you. The following plays are designed to bring out your truest desires and will be being to conceive your dream.

PLAY 3-1: Bucket List

Concept Practiced: Imagination Stimulation

PLAY 3-1: List 10 things you want to have, do, or experience before you leave this life.

> **SAMPLE PLAY 3-1**
>
> *Before I leave this world I will learn to fly, travel the ten top beaches of the world, and become a best-selling international author.*

1. _____
2. _____
3. _____
4. _____
5. _____
6. _____
7. _____
8. _____
9. _____
10. _____

PLAY 3-1: Make a statement that includes the top three things that you want to do before you leave this life. For those of you who have done this before, you will be delighted in doing this again, since you will realize how many of those things you listed previously have already come to pass. You may update or create your "bucket list statement to include your top three items now.

PLAY 3-2: The Eulogy

Concept Practiced: Imagination Stimulation

PLAY 3-2: Write Your Own Eulogy—in 10 words or less. Write what you would love for your eulogy to say!

> **SAMPLE PLAY 3-2**
>
> *Here lies so and so...He/she diligently paid all the bills on time.*

PLAY 3-3: Genie Grants 3

Concept Practiced: Imagination Stimulation

PLAY 3-3: A genie grants you three wishes:

> **SAMPLE PLAY 3-3**
>
> *I wish to be healthy, wealthy, and wise.*

1. _____

2. _____

3. _____

Summary of Conceive Section

Concept Practiced: Imagination Stimulation

Select a dream area from below. Refer to Chapter 4 in the course book for details.

- **S**-Space
- **E**-Energy
- **L**-Love
- **F**-Finance

Write a simple dream statement in 15 words or less in the present tense regarding a dream objective selected from one of these categories. You will input the dream statement into your ***Dream Plan Book.***

> **CONCEIVE SUMMARY PLAY**
>
> *LOVE CATEGORY*
>
> *I meet the love of my life, and we are perfectly matched and harmoniously compatible.*

My 15-Word Dream Statement _____

SECOND QUARTER: BELIEVE

Chapter 4:
The College Stage

> Overall, the University of Illinois college experience was as it should be – a developmental one, setting the stage for my life's dreams to be realized. With every dream, focussed action is needed to move the dream from the thinking stuff onto the stage of your life. With this college degree, I had earned my ticket out of the ghetto to step onto the world stage where I wanted to live.

During the early portion of my high school career, I slowly began learning about the college scholarship process. Outstanding students and ex-athletes from Edwardsville would return and tell us they were attending one school or another and that the institution paid for their expenses.

I found this amazing, but also realized there was a factor, which might eliminate me from similar outcomes. Gov felt we were as talented, or more talented, than many of those people, but they were also white.

Coach Lucco was always encouraging. He'd always repeat, "Stay out of trouble. Stay away from white girls. Remain committed in the classroom and you'll receive the big scholarships." He was right, but a strange message non-the-less. Mainly because in high school and college – we didn't see many black girls (only 3-4 in our graduation class) and we seldom pursued even the innocent friendship advances of white girls.

By my junior year, recruiters were contacting me and by the following winter, the pressure was intense. Some schools backed away when they learned I was black, but I still received over 100 inquiries/offers. I heard it all. An offer might include a car, clothes, cash, and a good job for my father.

Because of its proximity to Edwardsville, Govoner wanted to attend the University of Illinois. Distant places seemed more attractive to me. Kansas had Wilt Chamberlain intercede on its behalf. There was contact with UCLA, which at that time was an up and coming program. After much contemplation, I committed to Seton Hall then Marquette.

Govoner however, was going nowhere but Illinois and that later became my determining factor. I knew there would be difficulties no matter where I enrolled and we provided a significant amount of support for each other. I have always felt that with Gov, making it through those times was a lot more tolerable. After meeting the players at the various College recruiting me, I knew also with Gov, we would continue to be winners. We had nearly 15 years together and developed our own rules and language that allowed us to shut out the rest of the world and stay focused on what we needed to accomplish. We had also witnessed how swiftly our special world could be inverted.

On summer weekends, we would congregate with others on outdoor basketball courts in Indianapolis, Edwardsville, Alton, Chicago, Peoria, Memphis, New York, and in East St. Louis for exhibitions that sometimes drew large crowds. There, we let it all hang out. Spectators were always amazed by what they saw. A personal gimmick of mine as I got older, was to jump over cars or to brush my head against the rim as I dunked the ball. Govoner had an amazing shooting range – 20-25 feet, smooth as silk. I learned the car jumping routine from watching Olympic high jumper Ernie Haisley from Jamaica. I later mastered it and used it regularly while traveling with the Globetrotters. I never achieved the long jump like Haisley, but getting over the tip was enough to remain safe.

After these summer games, we'd hear what a great performance it was – "the best they had ever seen." One night, two carloads of us were driving home from East St. Louis, feeling full of ourselves, stopped to get something to drink. The place was a dive and several customers recognized us, asking for autographs. Finally, I approached the bar and ordered Cokes to go. "Get the fuck out of here," said the bartender. He then reached under the bar, pulled a gun, pointed it at my face and said, "I want you out of here now, along with all those other niggers, get out of my parking lot, or I'll blow your fucking head off."

The place got very quiet and still. We slowly backed out the door, got into the car and drove off. No one said a word about the incident on the drive home, nor have we discussed it since. But, the bond created by those experiences is difficult to sever.

Gov and I enrolled at Illinois. We joined another high school teammate Don Ohl to become the first time that three high school teammates started and lead scoring on a Big Ten team. Ohl was a very special human being and a great teammate. He later played in the NBA and by any measure, should be a Hall of Famer.

Govoner and I were the first two blacks to play basketball for the University of Illinois and there probably weren't more than 15-20 of us in the entire Big Ten Conference. By 1960, every team in the conference had one or two black players. In my first game at the college level, I scored 26 points for a sold out-crowd, and at 17 years old, I was thrilled! Howie Braun, an assistant coach, called me over and got in my face. "That was horrible. All you colored guys know is jumping and shooting. You won't play here doing that." He threatened me with saying that I must get 10+ assists and 10+ rebounds if I wanted to continue as a starter. Then he shut me off when I responded that I'd been a shooter and scorer and a winner all my life. I tried to remind him that this team averages 100 plus points per game, and everyone has a "green light." He just looked at me and asked, "You got yours tonight, but did you help anyone other than yourself?" His intent was mean-spirited at the time, but now as a practice to keep myself humble, I ask myself that same question often

We had many good players, but our head coach at this point in his career, had quit working hard and we didn't develop into the team we should have been. Two years later I was still struggling to find my new basketball role, my averages I'm told were: points 16, assists 9, and rebounds 8 – good enough for 1st team all Big Ten but not enough to attract big professional offers. Not until I got to New York playing for Coach Hank Rosenstein did I finally get it. As it turns out Howie was right – he just had this strange way of delivering a negative and critical message. My New York teammates, Frank Keith and Jim Daniels, were prototype East Coast point guards and I struggled to adapt. I played decently but I missed Gov and I missed being the team leader. It felt like I was starting all over and not like an all Big Ten veteran.

It eventually didn't matter anymore, I was 21 and I had expanded my vision and wanted to be the leading scorer and point guard for a Fortune 500 company. That was my new dream.

I began exploring possibilities. I remembered my junior year, Kroger had come onto campus promoting their management-training program. The night before I was to take their test, I asked a young lady administering the exam to have dinner with me. She had anticipated that I might ask for a copy of the test and before I did, she handed me one.

The next day, I purposely missed a single question – didn't want a perfect score to arouse suspicion. I missed ONLY one.

Several times I phoned Kroger's headquarters to see how I had done, but could not get an answer other than, "We're still processing them." Finally, through the mail came a reply. They had room for only a few well-qualified students – translation in those days meaning white, male students – with the best test scores. My test score fell below their standards. "Apply again." By then, I was beginning to understand the system. Illinois wanted me for basketball and little else.

We couldn't be in fraternities. There were only a few dorms in which we could live. We were seldom invited into the campus culture. Another reality began sinking in - there might be no life as I had came to know it after basketball and Illinois. Racism and the realities of life in Southern Illinois were beginning to be very real and visible to me. It was odd– racism was everywhere, but no one was a racist. In fact, most people were offended to even talk about it.

Until that time, I hadn't socialized much with co-eds and seldom dated. At Illinois, I did meet and spend time with a young black lady who was another positive influence in my life. She came from a middle class background – her father was a teacher in East St. Louis, Illinois – and we became close friends. I learned a lot from her and enjoyed her honesty and candor. Even though her father was wary of the fact that I was an athlete, we remained friends. Later in life, she became an assistant dean and the lessons learned from this beautiful 18 year old and her family have never been forgotten.

One of my happiest moments in college was being elected captain of the University's varsity team, and I was nervous with excitement. The first person I called was my dad–he understood more than I at the time, how significant this would be later in life. He told me he was proud and closed by saying, "go out and earn it, prove them right."

The only thing that would have been better would be to have Gov elected co-captain. I was excited to have earned the designation. I can't explain the rush I felt. But even this simple achievement was dashed by racial insensitivity. For one thing, two of the assistant coaches looked at each other in my presence and asked, "How are we going to explain this vote?" And seriously asked me, "How would you feel about stepping aside?"

I was invited to a private meeting in which the top assistant coach explained the pressures of his job to me. He suggested I extend the offer to one of my white teammates under the guise that the State of Illinois and "my people" would applaud my good judgment. To this, I said quickly, "No, thanks!!" He also realized that one of the honors bestowed upon the Illinois high school state tournament queen was to be escorted to the annual tournament by the newly elected Illinois varsity basketball captain. He said, "Imagine a 17-year-old, white, beauty queen holding hands and smiling in public and appearing in the next day's newspaper with an African-American. It just wouldn't be right." In fact, others chimed in, "for years to come, this young woman would be embarrassed and permanently scarred."

I felt bad, but I didn't budge! Forty years later in New York at a Globetrotters game, I had the opportunity to ask this former beauty queen, Jeanie Evers, who was from Aurora, Illinois, what she remembered and how she felt that night. She said she was thrilled and had the time of her life. I have never forgotten her and never regretted the experience. On the one hand, it did indeed bother me on a personal level. Yet, it made me more aware of the potential for good and bad in people and how the judgments of leaders are often ill conceived and transparent to their own ignorance, self- interests and personal issues.

Others at Illinois who were influential included Dave Downey, a great friend and a successful lawyer and business tycoon today who managed to give me respectful insights and life lessons every time we meet. Another was Jerry Colangelo, a teammate who transferred from Kansas and became owner of the Phoenix Suns and Arizona Diamondbacks. Jerry was probably the first white person who seriously discussed the flaws in the social system with Gov and me from his prospective. Jerry was a unique person and a breath of fresh air. He did not distance himself from us after basketball. We were always welcome to come to his frat house to meet, study and listen to music. I remember, at the time, he had an obsession for Frank Sinatra and Dean Martin tunes, which Gov and I never quite appreciated. My response to people who ask me about Colangelo is that he is smart, tough, fair, and truly authentic, a life-long friend who has not forgotten where we came from, as well as what the words "team" and "loyalty" means.

It was during these college years that I met the Reverend Jesse Jackson, a top quarterback candidate out of North Carolina who had been recruited by the U of I football team. While it was the beginning of a lifelong friendship, Jesse was already light years ahead of us. He was different and special. He knew there were harsh realities ahead for us to deal with during and after college. He was smarter than most of the coaches and wouldn't allow them to threaten him, pep talk him or con him. Jesse could not accept the system at Illinois. He left Illinois and became a standout student and All-Star at North Carolina A & T. His actions and assess ments of social situations at an early age still amaze me. I eventually would earn first and second team *All-Big Ten* and *All-American* mention and honors. Gov and I brought a different style to the game, not one readily accepted by many. Some of the same racial taunts we heard in high school followed us in college.

No place though was worse than Kentucky. Illinois because Illinois had black players. We couldn't play Kentucky in Lexington, so they scheduled the game at the Fairgrounds in Louisville during a year in which Kentucky held the nation's number one ranking. While we were in Louisville the entire team decided to go to a movie, and Gov and I were turned away at the door. Several teammates offered to leave with us including our team manager Dennis Swanson who raised holy hell with the theater manager. Most of our teammates were in total shock. But since we had these kind of experiences years earlier we knew our time would come on the basketball court and someone was going to pay.

In these moments Gov and I didn't need to say a word to each other about the situation, we knew what our job was and our reason for being there and it wasn't about a movie or another ignorant and bigoted movie manager. Gov and I walk away saying everything was cool and found our way to the ghetto and great food, some incredible live music and several new friends. At halftime of the big game, we were actually manhandling the Kentucky Wildcats and I had already scored 19 points. Their coach was furious. He was all over the officials and because the crowd was in such a frenzy everything we did was cheered loudly as he was obviously intimidating the officials.

Five minutes into the second half, I was out of the game after picking up a fifth foul. As I left the floor, the Kentucky's band played a chorus of a southern racially insensitive song. The rest of the game, we had police stationed behind our bench. Gov had the final shot with just seconds remaining. If he makes the shot, it's the biggest upset of the year. He missed and to this day I'd bet anything that the best shooter I've ever seen would knock down that simple 25-foot jumper. We lost and later just winked at each other as we crawled through an obscene crowd – we had done our job and helped awakened the South to a new day in college sports.

My college years were not a time overflowing with fond memories. When I returned to campus in 1994 to receive an alumni award, it was only my second visit to the school in over 30 years.

Overall, the college experience was as it should be – a developmental one, setting the stage for my life's dreams to be realized. In 2006, I was invited to joined the University of Illinois Foundation and my family was fortunate enough to be able to make a contribution of $2M that was designated to students needing financial support, mentoring and coaching. The hope is that minorities like myself, first generation students, and other first generation high potential students would not get lost in the crowd, and not be allowed to reach their full potential. The same education goal I had in high school was to "get by" was because no one cared. I knew I was smart, but somehow learning didn't matter. Because of President Joe White, Bruce Webber, and former Coach Lou Henson, I felt I should forgive and forget all the slights and bad experiences and focus on the possibilities and the good. I always remembered my own experience; I felt lost and without purpose because except for basketball I did not feel a need to be on campus.

As important as the University Illinois was to me, I still remember walking across a campus of 15-20,000 students and feeling absolutely alone and invisible. To this day, I wonder what it must feel like to be a real college student. Coach John McClendon was right. He predicted the challenging nature of my college experience at Illinois, during the time he was trying to recruit me to his historically black Tennessee State University.

The Mannie Jackson Leadership program was created to motivate and encourage the high potential student and has received national awards for its unique approach to student coaching and mentoring. My thanks go out to the ingenuity and dedication of Sherri White, PhD candidate and Dean Tanya Gallagher.

Putting everything in context, my university experience was invaluable and has meant a lot to my family and career. I shudder when I remind myself of my thought of leaving early and not taking advantage of this college stage. It one of the very few ways available to get my ticket for real independence.

With every dream, focused action is needed to move the dream from the thinking stuff to overcoming barriers and onto the stage of life. With my college degree, I earned my ticket out of the ghetto to step onto the bigger stage where I wanted to live. What is your ticket out of the ghetto of your life? Let's have some fun with the next *dreams to reality* step to learn how you can set the stage for your dream to come into reality. With that in mind, let's move on to S*tep 4, Stage Your Dream.*

Step 4:
Stage Your Dream

<u>*Concept Practiced: Visualization Expressed*</u>

To make it believable, stage your dream using your favorite visualization styles; collect dream elements for your dream script; by speaking, thinking, and practicing pieces of your dream, and lastly, by investing high level self-energy to build momentum to spin your dream into reality!

Congratulations! You have completed the CONCEIVE section of this workbook, and you have conceived and written a simple 15-word dream statement. With Step 4 we introduce the BELIEVE section of The Playbook.

Now it's time to make it believable! The purpose of this step is to strengthen and enhance your dream statement with belief. To build belief, your dream statement enters a stage, your **Dream Plan Book.** Your dream is attracted to you by giving it a visualized form. Some find it easy to form a picture in their mind's eye. Others do not.

Some are visually oriented; still others can feel the wind in their hair as they imagine themselves walking along that beach hand in hand with the love of their life. They are kinesthetic. Whatever dream you have, you will find your own way of presenting it to your mind's eye. Enlightened visualization is the concept of identifying the visualization style that best resonates with you.

Your visualization will build on your dream statement, with details from your dream elements; to include photos, artwork, and quotes, to build your *published dream script*.

To hold your vision, you will practice speaking, thinking, and even rehearsing your dream, as well as adding the energy momentum and action strategy to bring it about.

To stage your dream you will first discover your most natural styles of expression. Then you will go on field trips, interviews, and shopping jaunts.

PLAY 4-1: Uniquely You

Concept Practiced: Visualization Expressed

PLAY 4-1: Identify five unique things about you small or big.

> **SAMPLE PLAY 4-1**
>
> *Ever since I can remember, I have always been good at reading, writing, and communications! I love to read and write; especially writing.*

1. _____

2. _____

3. _____

4. _____

5. _____

PLAY 4-1: Choose one or two key things that are unique about you and about which you are also passionate_____

PLAY 4-2: Visualization Style

Concept Practiced: *Visualization Expressed*

PLAY 4-2: Number your expressive and visualization style below in order of preference, with 1 being your highest preference.

> **SAMPLE PLAY 4-2**
>
> Using Dream Statement: *I take an extensive, intimate month-long journal to Italy's top five cities.*
>
> Visual: *Rent videos of Italy.*
>
> Verbal/Auditory: *Play audio DVDs to learn to speak Italian.*
>
> Kinesthetic: *Take Italian cooking classes, shot at a local Italian grocery store and eat at Italian cafes.*
>
> Cognitive: *Study Italian History and Geography*

- [ ] Visual
- [ ] Auditory/Verbal
- [ ] Kinesthetic
- [ ] Cognitive

Different ways I can express, stimulate, and practice my Dream Statement.

Visual

Auditory/Verbal

Kinesthetic

Cognitive

PLAY 4-3: Dream Acting

Concept Practiced: *Visualization Expressed*

PLAY 4-3: Now that you have written your simple dream statement, and have some ideas how to visualize your dream, use this play to practice the bits and pieces of your dreams.

List on the next page activities that you can practice which will create the picture, thought, feeling, or idea of your dream statement.

SAMPLE PLAY 4-3

Using Dream Statement: *I find the love of my life and fall deeply in love.*

Visual: *I find photos of attractive people, body style, face style, etc.*

Verbal/Auditory: *I record a collection of my favorite romantic songs.*

Kinesthetic: *I learn salsa dancing or other romantic dance steps.*

Cognitive: *I read and study the latest, greatest relationship books.*

1 _____

2 _____

3 _____

4 _____

5 _____

6 _____

Ideas & thoughts of how I can Stage and Practice My Dream _____

_____

_____

_____

_____

_____

_____

Chapter 5:
Slam Dunking the Globetrotters Dream!

> *I was so numbed by the magic they wove, I found myself walking up to the founder, owner and coach, Abe Saperstein, and told him, "I would like to play for you guys." Abe patted me on the leg, and said, "Sure. When you're old enough, and have finished college, come see me."*

During the final year at Illinois, I had reason to believe basketball would furnish me with two fascinating opportunities in the immediate future. There was the prospect of making the Olympic team, which I hoped would then be followed by a pro career. In those days, the Harlem Globetrotters were too popular and too good and seemed an impossibility except for the fact that Saperstein had promised me a look after graduation when Mr. Brownstein had tried to recruit me out of high school. The odds were not great for the NBA, for different reasons like racial quotas, geography, and exposure. The only blacks that could be heard saying NBA basketball was not walled off by race in the 50's and 60's were those few black players who were selected.

The Hall of Fame 1960 U.S. Olympic team was among our best ever, including Oscar Robertson, Jerry West, Jerry Lucas, Walt Bellamy and Terry Dischinger, among others. I was optimistic of my chances during the team's formative stages. I was All-Big Ten, and honorable mention All-American, had excelled in the trials and had expected an invitation.

While waiting for a plane ticket to arrive, I learned I had been replaced, by a player who later went on to have a great NBA career, but the fact that I was eliminated shocked me to the point where I lost focus. I later joined the New York Tuck Tapers, a National Industrial League team.

What I discovered after college were scores of black athletes, all better prepared than me with nowhere to go. There was no International, no minor league, only 8 or 9 NBA teams and a seemingly loaded Globetrotters' roster with an owner who was now angered by my decision to stay in New York.

Although some may disagree today because it wasn't an acknowledged policy with no governmental or media oversight, everyone close to the NBA knew the 10-team league operated under a quota system with 2 or 3 blacks per team.

The first time I saw the Globetrotters was at age 10 or 11 during an All-Star game on an outdoor court near St. Louis. I was so inspired by their magic, I found myself walking up to the founder, owner and coach, Abe Saperstein, and told him, "I would like to play for you guys."

Abe patted me on the shoulder and said, "Sure. When you're old enough and after you graduate college, come see me."

Five years later, as a high school senior, I was contacted by one of their recruiters. The Globetrotters had attracted attention by signing a few high school stars like the great J.C. Gibson from Los Angeles and a young-hearted player named Hicks; and developed them into box office hits.

When Abe discovered I had been targeted to bypass college, he was furious. Abe was a resident of Chicago and close friend of Doug Mills, then the athletic director at the University of Illinois. He knew the school was after me. Abe told me to go to college, get a degree, and then see him afterwards when there would be a spot for me on the Globetrotters.

He stayed in touch while I played at Illinois. Soon after I graduated I was with the Tuck Tapers, having a great time in New York learning how to play point guard, and hopeful that the New York Knicks would eventually offer an NBA opportunity.

When it became obvious that the NBA was not interested, I again contacted Abe. He told me to obtain a passport, report to team headquarters in Chicago, Illinois. I left soon thereafter for Europe as a proud member of the Harlem Globetrotters. I was on Cloud 9, beside myself on an Alitalia jet to London and 30+ countries after that. It was like a flick of the switch, sitting with Meadowlard Lemon, JC Gipson, Ernie Wagner, Murphy Summons, a 6'5 point guard from Detroit), an All-American from Indiana Hallie Bryant and "Tex" Harrison. We were proud and we were good.

The experience was enriched immeasurably because Abe decided to join the team for the tour. He made me one of the team's featured players and spent a great deal of personal time with me. Photos of the two of us were taken at the Berlin Wall, in Paris, Brussels and at a former Polish concentration camp where I learned from Abe, who was Jewish, about the suffering of another race of people.

Abe would talk to me for hours about how he promoted and marketed the team, how he had made it one of the most famous products in the world. He repeated over and over "We are the ones who have introduced this game around the world, and we are the State Department ambassadors...no one beats us and no one entertains better – that's why we draw fans from all walks of life all over the world." Abe was great and made it obvious that he thought I was something more than just a player, and that there was a future for me in the organization beyond on-the-court basketball. He showed me reports where the team defeated the world champion Lakers and in 1958 his team drew 4 million people worldwide and mostly all games were sell-outs. Many of the games we played on our European tour were in very large soccer stadiums and we prepared ourselves daily to play and entertain.

We certainly were never overpaid. My college teammate was making just $8,800 a year as a starter in the NBA, but to me the $12,000+ for the Globetrotters and what I was experiencing, justified the decision to be happy as a Globetrotter.

When we landed in London that May, it was the first time I had touched foreign soil. That remains a thrill frozen in time. We would eventually appear in many beautiful countries, including Russia, Africa, and the Middle East. We played national teams on every stop and those were extremely serious games and we always won, usually with ease. Abe would slip me extra cash after each game and say, "thank you." All of us loved to play, especially games against NCAA and NBA teams, and the hotly competitive and ever-popular College All-Star series, the second time I played with Hall of Famer Connie Hawkins. It was magical...the crowds, Connie, and the competition.

Those Globetrotter teams included Hallie Bryant, Govner Vaughn, Ernie Waggoner, Bobby Jo Mason, "Tex" Harrison, the team "fireball" comic Meadowlark Lemon, Connie Hawkins and J.C. Gipson - the signature performers for years. Meadowlark and I were roommates for a time and became friends. I learned much about Meadowlark that would surprise those familiar with him only through his antics on the court.

In most of Europe, we found a refreshingly different attitude toward race. The only places we would encounter racial animosity were on U.S. military bases. We could eat where we what we wanted and see whatever women we wanted. That sort of freedom caused several minor altercations with military personnel.

It was in Russia and behind the Iron Curtain that I found myself answering questions I never publicly addressed. I found myself in the position of defending American-styled capitalism and democracy to people who wanted to know if racism was as brutal and extreme in the United States as they had been told and if so, why was it tolerated in a so-called "free society." They would ask me: "Why can't you vote? Why segregated education? Why no public access?"

I often mingled with college students to exchange views and experiences. For that liberty, I once found myself in Abe's "dog house" and in a Hungarian retention center for several hours. I guess exercising my freedom of speech and first amendment rights were not always appreciated. I truly believe it was in those moments that I became a die-hard Capitalist. As in most cases, I would win the debate. I'd always close with, *we aren't perfect, but can you aspire to lead your nation?*

A couple months later in Finland, I was invited into a Finnish home to spend the night. We talked until daybreak. It was a warm experience with a delightful family, with whom for years I maintained contact.

Globetrotter life, though, could also be debilitating. One played 250 games a year, much of the travel was by bus, leaving the arena late at night to be in another city for the next afternoon game or promotion. It was so much fun we hardly noticed the time passing or the travel. I'm always asked, "How those Converse all-stars shoes held up through several hundred games and playing conditions. Well, thick socks along with a little cardboard, very strong callous feet, strong ankles and dependable knees were essential. I heard that Meadowlark never missed a game in 20+ years. I believe it; he was a very unusual physical specimen and very dedicated. Whatever he was paid, which was a lot – he earned it big time! I also often heard it said by the old timers, that he was a knock-off of Goose Tatum and "Showboat" Hall. That didn't matter to me, he was special.

My goal was to be featured as a fancy dribbler and finisher, the latter meaning that I was expected to explode off the floor and complete plays with spectacular slam-dunks. I wasn't very special at either of these. But I soon found out what both of those roles do to a person's knees and legs in a short time. I had money (saved 100% of what I earned) and confirmed Albert Einstein's theory that the most amazing phenomena in math is compound interest, I had a little celebrity and a great adventure. But it was time to think of moving on to the next phase of life.

My body clock told me very early this would not be a long career, because I wasn't driven or motivated to train or take the pain. However, at age 25, I had no interest in becoming a basketball vagabond and had my sights set on bigger accomplishments. From the moment I first spoke of my basketball ambition to Abe Saperstein at the age of 12, I wrote my Harlem Globetrotters dream script, which had now come to pass. Now needed to write and new plan and script and move on to another one! But wait, before I go any further in my story, let me stop and have my friend Deborah Nelson show you how to write your own personal dream script in ***Step 5 – Pen Your Dream Script!***

Step 5:
Pen Your Dream Script

Concept Practiced: *The Power of Words—Write it!*

To transform vision into words is the most powerful step in the **dreams to reality process.** *Writing your dream script is simple. There are three parts. The beginning is your initial dream statement; the middle includes your detailed dream elements; and the end is the final proclamation of your dream in its fullness!*

By now, you are feeling inspired, creative, and motivated with many exciting and intuitive ideas stirring.

Now is the time to capture them. Feel the Power of the Pen, and with courage, move your dream forward right now!

The purpose of this step is to write the dream decree, dream script, and dream theme, to form the storyline of your Dream Plan Book.

With these three plays, you will embellish your simple dream statement in vivid detail by merging your dream elements with your dream statement to form your dream script.

This is where the rubber meets the road. This is the powerful moment where your dream begins to enter the physical word. This is where you put your pen to the paper. Here you are going to write you dream script or story. Be strong and courageous. Do not let fear overcome you. Write it! This is your unique story and your unique book. There is no right or wrong way to write it. Just be yourself!

Now that you have already written your dream statement, and collected your dream elements, the script is nearly written. The last part of writing the script is to combine your dream statement, with detailed dream elements, to form a final pronouncement of your dream.

PLAY 5-1: Dream Decree

Concept Practiced: *The Power of Words—Write it!*

PLAY 5-1: We begin with the end in mind. This play guides your dream story to the next level of reality. How is that? We start with Power of the Pen and enhance the dream with faith. Below write out the feelings, thoughts, and visual images you sense when you imagine the endpoint of your dream:

SAMPLE PLAY 5-1

Using Dream Statement:
I take an extensive, intimate month-long journal to Italy's Five Most Beautiful cities.

I decree that am falling in love with beautiful Italy!

Using Dream Statement:
I travel extensively to Romantic Italy for an entire summer with my special lady.

I decree that my the love of my life and I are Romantically charged on our Italian Journey; and it sets the stage is set for a successful proposal in marriage.

Images_____
_____
_____
_____
_____

Sounds_____
_____
_____
_____
_____

Feelings_____
_____
_____
_____
_____

Thoughts_____
_____
_____
_____
_____

My Dream Decree: You say it, you feel it, and you BELIEVE IT! Make a simple decree regarding the endpoint of your dream story. Begin with the end in mind. This dream decree will define the end of your dream. *You will input this dream decree as text near the end of your **Dream Plan Book**_____*
_____
_____
_____
_____

PLAY 5-2: Dream Theme

Concept Practiced: *The Power of Words—Write it!*

PLAY 5-2: The beginning and the middle of the script for your dream story are starting to take form and from this you can expect a theme or an inspiration to emerge. The theme is the emotional glue holds a story together.

Below are some themes that have emerged for **Dream Plan Books.**

This part is entirely unique and entirely personal, but here are some suggestions and titles of how dreams have been written in story format.

Journey to Italia!
Theme: Beauty

"100 days to My Most Beautiful Body"
Theme: Beauty

"My Perfect Day"
Theme: Perfection

"I Love My Job"
Theme: Purpose

"The Most Incredible Family on Earth"
Theme: Love

PLAY 5:2: Keeping in mind that a theme is the emotional glue and purpose for a dream come true, write a theme for your dream. This dream theme will be input into your *Dream Plan Book* forming the basis of the story plot.

> ### SAMPLE PLAY 5-2
>
> Using Dream Statement:
> *I take an extensive, intimate month-long journal to Italy's Five Most Beautiful cities.*
>
> *Theme: Beauty*
>
> Using Dream Statement:
> *I travel extensively to Romantic Italy for an entire summer with my special lady.*
>
> *Theme: Romance*

My Dream Theme _____

PLAY 5-3: Dream Elements

Concept Practiced: *The Power of Words—Write it!*

PLAY 5-3: Dream elements are collected in preparation to input and upload to your *Dream Plan Book*. These include poetry, quotes, photos, artwork, drawing, scanned images, etc. Write down the dream elements that you have collected and will collect to enhance your dream statement.

> **SAMPLE PLAY 5-3**
>
> Using Dream Statement: *I take an extensive, intimate month-long journal to Italy's Five Most Beautiful cities.*
>
> Dream Theme: *Beauty*
>
> Dream Decree: *My journey to Italy is a month-long intimate visit, which begins in Rome. The visit is to five beautiful cities, and we learn the language before and as we go.. Having a list of key Italian words and phases, we practice in our spare moments. In the end, I fall in love with Beautiful Italy with all my senses of sight, sound, taste, hearing and feeling! I am full of its beauty, its life, now fully knowing the Country of Italy. It touches me deeply and becomes a part of who I am.*

Visual Dream Elements _____

_____
_____
_____
_____
_____
_____
_____

Auditory/Verbal Dream Elements _____

_____
_____
_____
_____
_____
_____
_____

Kinesthetic Dream Elements _____

_____
_____
_____
_____
_____
_____
_____

Cognitive Dream Elements _____

_____
_____
_____
_____
_____
_____
_____

PLAY 5-3: Write a simple paragraph stating the beginning, middle and end of your *Dream Plan Book.* This dream script will form the basic outline for the text of your *Dream Plan Book.*

Dreams Script Paragraph_____

Chapter 6:
Basketball Dreams to Business Dreams

> *The breakthrough came while I was completing work on my MBA. Strong black-white relationships were rare at the time, but I had developed one through basketball with a man named John Watson. He had come to understand my anxieties, was sensitive to the obstacles I was confronting and eventually introduced me to his supervisor, an executive at General Motors Cadillac Division, Dr. Jim Oliver.*

As a National Industrial League team, the New York Tapers offered an advantage that most sports organizations did not. Many of the athletes were there exclusively for basketball, but the owner of the Technical Tape Corp., New Rochelle, NY's, Paul Cohen, would identify certain players he felt had the aptitude and personality to be of value in a business sense and offer them jobs outside the game. I discovered recently that several former All-Americans who joined the league in those days are still active executives with their companies.

I was fortunate to be one of those players selected. While playing for the team, I worked on the national customer service desk handling product issues from all over the country. Our products were mostly bulk sales of pressure sensitive tapes – masking, cellophane, and the stronger stuff. The contacts were usually by phone and I possessed the voice and a decidedly midwest diction that prevented callers from identifying me as black. All they knew was that I worked long hours and was adept at solving problems. In fact, I was successful to the point where I eventually taught a sales and service class for Mr. Cohen. I wasn't very good at it – but he loved my effort and how serious I took the assignment.

For me, the experience was an awakening. I realized I could function in the business world and much of my effort in the years immediately thereafter was an attempt to identify a satisfactory entry point. I wanted to be an entrepreneur like Paul Cohen. With late stage MS, he was physically handicapped, but sharp mentally – he was good person and wanted to help people achieve their dreams.

During my two separate stints with the Globetrotters, plus time in professional leagues, I was constantly sending resumes and interviewing, seeking either a position or inclusion in management training programs. At that time, an applicant was required to include a photo with each resume. One reason for this practice soon became apparent. Though I applied at a variety of levels, I systematically received standard rejection form letters that were so impersonal you felt like crap. Most just went unanswered. How were those Human Resource managers to know that a future Honeywell President, a future Fortune 500 board director, a successful hard driving entrepreneur and future Owner of the Harlem Globetrotters just wanted a chance?

What I gradually discovered was that – other than a few small eastern companies like Tuck Tape – people of color were seldom (overstatement intended) working at white-collar levels in American business. Most toiled in factories and other labor intensive positions. I met only one Advertising executive even though African Americans were buying cars, hair products, soft drinks, good whiskey, auto and other insurance at a rate of 30+ billion dollars per year, and no blacks employed. How do you explain that? The executives I met in Detroit was named Doug Alligood who was with the firm BBD&O and he was super good and brilliant. He moved around the office like Magic Johnson with a kick-ass attitude. One of his accounts was Pepsi Cola; and to this day if given a choice I always take Pepsi.

I did some substitute teaching in the basketball off-season, enough to learn that I loved it but it wasn't a final career choice for me. Not only is teaching hard work, but in inner-city schools you feel close to disaster every day. I dreamed of being rich and powerful enough to change this. I felt our youth deserved better. I eventually quit substitute teaching when I was hired by a discount shoe company on the south side of Chicago to work in one of its stores.

Something was wrong with this picture. I had a degree that was academically solid from a major university, had traveled the world; and I felt qualified and committed to doing more.

Meanwhile, I'd meet white ex-college classmates who were moving along nicely with major corporations. As I began to understand there was a racial fence between me and the type of successful business future I had envisioned, my initial response was anger – deep anger. For the first time, I began taking a really hard look at the hard-core civil rights movement. Jesse Jackson had been right all along. Education alone was neither the problem nor the answer. At age 23 I felt trapped, totally embarrassed and ashamed of my country and its promises not kept.

There were no front office jobs in sports and since my body had no intention of me becoming a career Harlem Globetrotter, the phase of my life where athletics were a sustaining focus was approaching the finish line.

The scene around me was both confusing and terrifying. Black contemporaries were becoming coaches, teachers, postal workers, truck drivers or inmates. I began to recall words of Howard Popham – the old golf "pro" from my hometown – was he right? Had I wasted my time and dreams? Black athletes who had not received degrees ignored declining sports skills and attempted to hang on to flimsy minor league careers. Some were already falling off the side and back to street life.

I was determined not to panic. My family didn't know my fears, and remained supportive. They always said, "you'll find a way you always do, there is plenty of time." I began taking graduate courses. And because of my science aptitude I tested for a government grant as a National Science Fellow and was accepted. I was certain this new credential would influence corporate thinking as to my competence. But as just one example; when I answered an advertisement that offered entry level management training with the Rexall Company in St. Louis, where I felt I was known, I was tested, interviewed around, then shown the revolving door after talking for hours rehashing basketball stories.

Those transitional years were the most difficult of my life. Out of college, one discovers you are on your own and small missteps or bad choices often influence a lifetime. Life was not basketball where you shoot a ball 30 times and make 15 and you were a hero. Nor could you simply turn the page to the next game. Every shot and every decision seemed to count. I had to learn to understand risk and losses. Many assumed I had it all and would ask – why should I be so conservative and concerned. After all, I had youth, cash in the bank, new cars, and a college degree… this all seemed to be trumped by being the wrong color. That was both my obsession and my view of life at the time.

Those were the late Vietnam years and although I was not drafted, the concern that the draft was just around the corner was always with me. I even entered into a marriage to a nice bright women that would last a few years. This too was a product of fear and my search for stability. I was facing some of life's most difficult realities from which I couldn't run, jump, or shoot over. My knees were getting worse and the special services guys who offered me just about everything to join the military in a special publicity pre-game ceremony in Chicago Stadium eventually turned their backs.

The big breakthrough came while I was working on an MBA at the University of Detroit. Strong black-white relationships were rare at the time, but I developed one through basketball with a young guy named John Watson, now Dr. John Watson. He is the only person I ever met who on two occasions out ran me baseline to baseline on the basketball court.

The following is an excerpt from a letter written by Dr. John Watson, March 22, 2011 who recently passed away on April 17. 2011.

I remember playing basketball at the local gym when Mannie came into play. They asked me to guard him. His first run down the court, he hit and 18-foot jumper. The next time, he dunked right over me.

At the time, I was working in the Cadillac division of GM. Mannie was looking for a job after trying out for a couple of NBS teams (NY Knicks and Detroit Pistons). He was close to making the teams in both cities, but back then, the teams had quotas and he was the third best African American and only the top two could make the team.

I told him he should come by my work to interview. He said, "They'd never hire a black guy," and I told him the hiring was all based on tests. The next day, he came to GM and tested in my division with one of the highest Wonderlic scores the administrator had even seen. Mannie worked fro me until we were both transferred to the labor and relations division where we became equals.

In the late 60's during the Detroit riots, my wife and I lived nearby the action. We decided to leave for our Port Huran lakehouse. We invited Mannie and his wife to join us. It was getting really dangerous both in the neighborhood and at work. Mannie wouldn't go due to looting and on principle. He said, "I'm going to stay on my floor with a gun and shoot any who comes in."

When the riots were over, I was playing recreational ball with Mannie and Gov Vaughn. I was the only white guy in the gym and I didn't really want to go in. Mannie said I'd be ok to go in and play since I was with him. And he was right. I actually got a standing ovation for going in that gym that day. Thanks to Mannie.

Without any pretension, John Watson became my angel. His family and mine weathered the Detroit riots together and shared fears that our world was coming apart. Our two families were bonded by a social crisis through the game of basketball. He had come to understand my anxieties, was sensitive to the obstacles I was confronting and eventually introduced me to his supervisor, a senior executive at General Motors Cadillac Division, Dr. Jim Oliver.

Dr. Oliver was a clinical psychologist at the Cadillac car division (GM's premier location) and had devised a series of tests for people seeking management careers with General Motors. Warned that the tests were exhausting and difficult, I was anxious to take them anyway. These tests were heralded as predictors of success and scientifically validated by GM's elite upper management teams. GM believed that corporate leaders had to be something like a minimum of 130% smarter (test scores) than those they supervised. I never believed it then and I don't now. After informing me that my score of 40+ was exceptional, Dr. Oliver asked if I had cheated. Unconvinced with my denial, he retested me, and I scored a 44.

Dr. Oliver eventually hired me to administer those tests and oversee the apprenticeship program for skill trade worker/new hires. As he took me around to meet officers in the company, Dr. Oliver invariably would introduce me as, "Mannie Jackson, the young colored guy with the 44 Wonderlic." He was both fascinated and pleased by the fact that someone with my background could master his tests. I knew he was proud of me and he tolerated all my inexperience and flaws. I liked him and we got along great and work in his department was a pleasure. Working with Dr. Oliver and John Watson, I soon realized how limited I was and how hard I would have to work just to keep up.

The GM job and that experience was my big start in business, but unfortunately it was an area that failed to hold my interest. I wanted management and leadership responsibilities. I wanted to make a lot of money. I wanted to make policy and to change corporate America. I also knew there were dozens of black guys my equal or better who hadn't yet met their "John Watson." John became a very close friend and we made a good working team. It wasn't long thereafter, we were both promoted to the Labor Relations Division. After recruiting and administering the test for 18 months – I could do it in my sleep and could predict test success like I could predict the final scores of a game. And I was usually 70% right if I could speak to an applicant for just 30 minutes.

In my free time when not playing basketball or going to University of Detroit classes, I'd attend amateur fights at Cobo Hall and the Brewster Center in Detroit. This was fun for me because I wanted to learn to box and I loved meeting fighters and fight fans. Hanging out with Ray Scott the Detroit Piston's Coach and former player and the fight clubs' owner – I also thought it would be interesting to one day market the fight business.

Detroit had the best fight clubs in the nation, and one night I met a young man named Hedgemon Lewis – after 30 minutes, I invited him to come to GM to take the test to see what would happen. Most of the boxers were hip, hardcore, street kids – usually very mean and very skilled as fighters but easy to get to know. I thought to myself, *several of these young guys were really intelligent.* When Hedgemon showed up at the office, eyebrows were raised. Sure enough, I administered Dr. Oliver's modified Adaptability Intelligence test and struck gold. Hedgeman scored a 49+ plus, compared to Oliver's perfect 58 and my 50. I remember he also scored high on the Wonderlic, the Adaptability, and the Dilford-Zimmerman. The typical plant general foreman would score in the mid 30's. He left the office, but Dr. Oliver wanted to see him and talk with him again. Since this completely shattered the corporate paradigm, Oliver wanted to know more.

Six months later, Lewis resurfaced in Los Angeles, managed by actor Ryan O'Neal, fighting on national television for the welterweight championship of the world – Oliver, Watson, and I talked for hours one night about the wasted African-American intellectual asset. I immediately thereafter wanted to know about the possibilities of my owning a business starting with a Cadillac dealership. Lewis inspired me less with his scores but more with his social quotient and conviction to lead and grow. This was my personal breakthrough that vaulted me on offense again. I was fired up – I was in active dream mode and my game was just beginning, and with no more fear; I felt like I was on fire!

Some months later, I found my way to Minneapolis as a representative of the automobile industry to speak on one of General Motors' pet topics – white-collar unionism. With Dr. Oliver as a mentor, I was well versed on this subject and the presentation went splendidly.

Afterwards, the Honeywell Corporation and Control Data, who asked if I had any interest in relocating. It was just the breakthrough that I had hoped. Sometimes we can feel stuck and hitting dead ends with no movement towards our dreams. One of my favorite quotes is,

"A curve in the road is not the end of the road; if you prepare yourself and energize your psyche, most likely it will become a new and exciting beginning, if you make the turn." During my questions and answer phase of Minneapolis speech, I mentioned my career aspiration and dreams. A senior Honeywell executive apparently heard me as did my first Honeywell supervisor, Fran Miller.

Before I go on with the rest of the story, let's relocate to the next step to learn how to create the laser focus and momentum needed for your dream to reach its breakthrough. Step out of the mundane to do a little work to fire up energy and build momentum in order to shift your dream from belief to action with *Step 6, Set Your Own Dream on Fire!*

Step 6:
Set Your Dream On Fire

<u>Concept Practiced:</u> *Ignite Dream Momentum*

Formula for Dream Momentum:

Hold steady a magnifying glass to direct a beam of light to spark up tiny pieces of dry grass. With a prepared strategy, you are able to ignite the kindling, which fuels large logs able to produce massive heat energy. All this started with a sliver of sunlight and a simple magnifying glass.

Dream step starts with pure desire (sliver of light) directed through a magnifying glass (faith) onto dry twigs (thinking stuff). Write a dream statement, (spark); add dream script, (kindling); fuel with self-energy, (large logs) to create such dream momentum, and set the dream on Fire!

Momentum is the unstoppable spinning force that once started, produces a power of its own.

It is so powerful that pure momentum without friction has been theorized to create perpetual motion. The purpose of this step is to energize you to follow through with creating your ***Dream Plan Book.***

Energize your dream statement, dream theme, dream decree, dream script and your developing dream story, by investing personal energy with action to give it life! Spin your dream to life. Continual practice of thoughts that enhance your self-energy will build momentum for your dream.

Getting momentum started requires an initial investment of energy, and the more focused the energy the better. To invest energy a belief structure must be present. Use energy to add action to your dream!

You have created the dream statement, dream elements, and dream decree. These next plays guide you to practice building self-energy and to focus that self-energy on your envisioning your dream, to give your dream more belief, more energy, and more momentum.

Limit the friction that you experience and maximize your self-energy in the form of physical, spiritual, and mental energy.

You may choose to spend physical, spiritual, and mental energy or you can invest it. Develop awareness in choosing between energy investment or energy depletion.

PLAY 6-1: Self-Energy

Concept Practiced: *Ignite Dream Momentum*

PLAY 6-1: Select the top 5 states that energize you the most and number them in order of highest self-energy level created.

> **SAMPLE PLAY 6-1**
>
> *My 5 most energizing states*
>
> *1. Thankfulness*
>
> *2. Inspiration*
>
> *3. Creativity*
>
> *4. Joy*
>
> *5. Bliss*

To check off the items, click in the desired boxes then click to the right of the words to enter the order of specific numbers. Continued on next page.

- ☐ Peace
- ☐ Frustration
- ☐ Desperation
- ☐ Anger

- [ ] Joy
- [ ] Honor
- [ ] Acceptance
- [ ] Bliss
- [ ] Enlightenment
- [ ] Love
- [ ] Guilt
- [ ] Inspiration
- [ ] Creativity
- [ ] Rest
- [ ] Revenge
- [ ] Jealousy
- [ ] Reason
- [ ] Grief
- [ ] Fear
- [ ] Pride
- [ ] Desire
- [ ] Courage
- [ ] Apathy

PLAY 6-2: Focus on the Ball

Concept Practiced: *Ignite Dream Momentum*

PLAY 6-2: List states from play 6-1 in order of energy level and quality, from highest to lowest:

> **SAMPLE PLAY 6-2**
>
> *This week I noticed that frustration was a state repeatedly triggered while driving. I remind myself to "focus on the ball," and I change my focus to envisioning the next step in making my dream for a new career to be realized. My energy is invested in my dream, rather than in the frustration of how people drive. I realize that over time, this energy invested brings me closer to what I want, than what I don't want.*

1 _____   5 _____

2 _____   6 _____

3 _____   7 _____

4 _____   8 _____

9 _____   17 _____

10 _____   18 _____

11 _____   19 _____

12 _____   20 _____

13 _____   21 _____

14 _____   22 _____

15 _____   23 _____

16 _____   24 _____

PLAY 6-2: Practice this play by being aware of your states. Mark the states you feel this week, and train yourself to live in higher energy states. When you find yourself in energy deleting states, remind yourself to "focus on the ball!"

This requires continuous practice; but conserves energy for a focused investment, rather than thoughtless expenditure of unproductive emotional energies. Invest energy and action in your dreams.

PLAY 6-3: Dream Momentum

Concept Practiced: *Ignite Dream Momentum*

PLAY 6-3: Dream momentum shows up in bits and pieces entering the circumference of your life.

Dream momentum hastens events, people, situations attracted to your physical reality. You have created dream statements, dream elements, and dream decrees. You have been working with imagination and words. Now you will begin to see things starting to fill in your dream plan and strategies. Your dream is moving from the believing phase into the receiving phase.

Identify Momentum Elements—photos and graphics you have gathered for your *Dream Plan Book*.

SAMPLE PLAY 6-3

Using Dream Statement:
100 Days to My Most Fit Body

Momentum Elements:
In three weeks of steady training, I have lost 3 inches in my waist and 1 inch in the hips. I plan to increase momentum by stepping up the levels and weights in the workout.moments. In the end, I fall in love with Beautiful Italy with all my senses of sight, sound, taste, hearing and feeling! I am full of its beauty, its life, now fully knowing the Country of Italy. It touches me deeply and becomes a part of who I am.

List Momentum Elements below

1 _____
_____
_____

2 _____
_____
_____

3 _____
_____
_____

Identify how you may add energy and action to these elements entering your space to further increase momentum

1 _____
_____
_____

2 _____
_____
_____

3 _____
_____
_____

To add believability to my dream script and dream decree; I have collected the following photos, graphics, quotes and poetry:

THIRD QUARTER: RECEIVE

Chapter 7:

Honeywell Dream Well Done

> *Meanwhile, Honeywell had been calling and this time it was the CEO who set forth a guaranteed training and advancement program, one that was extremely appealing. Honeywell is a Fortune 120 corporation with annual sales exceeding $6 billion. There were eight different businesses operating under the holding company and an opportunity for young executives to move from one to another.*

General Motors provided my doorway to the corporate world, and executives at Honeywell were the ones who first offered the leadership program and advancement opportunities in line with my goals.

I left two great friends behind at GM, John Watson and Jim Oliver. I also left a dispute behind as to how the company would settle a long standing suggestion award I had earned. To GM's credit, my exit was professional and courteous and the award and its financial parameters exceeded my own expectations. For the first time in my life, I knew what financial security felt like. I have told only a few people the size of the award and the change it bought to General Motors. To this day I ask myself, *how could one person be do lucky?*

The way the award issue was settled after almost 10 years erased the distrust and negative feelings I had about the matter in which some GM's middle managers discussed and handled the riots. The "n-word" was overheard frequently and death threats were overheard as a strategy to protect the building and production line. I sat in every meeting I would try and calm emotions and fears that were spreading. One day, Dr. Oliver pulled me aside and said, "Your effort is gallant, but I am directing you to stay home and protect your family. This will all blow over and hopefully we'll be better off and some good will be found from all this." It was clear--he wanted me safe and he too, was very afraid.

So I made the transfer ("turn in the road") and went to Minnesota as went into immediate culture shock. In Detroit, I'd been immersed in the black community and post riot attitudes were still simmering. In Minneapolis, seeing a person of color on the streets in the evening was rare, a phenomenon that was not much different in the halls of the business world.

I'd made a conscious decision that my sports background would remain exactly that – in the background. I wanted a fresh start to be judged solely on my abilities and contributions as a business player. That pledge was honored. Years later when I became the out-front person in an ownership group that hoped to place an NBA franchise in San Diego, my former involvement with athletics became a media focus. Many longtime business associates were stunned. This was 1989 before Internet and Google.

My early experiences with Honeywell were frustrating mainly because of me, I was truly impatient. Grand assurances had dissolved into another meaningless job with the title of Director. I had held a more complex position while at Cadillac Motor Car Division at GM. Essentially, I was there to supply proof to the government investigators that the aerospace and defense segment of the company was in compliance with executive order 11246 and its equal opportunity demands.

So disappointing was this development, that I contacted a friend of a good friend, Hall-of-Famer Earl Lloyd, the first African-American to play in the NBA. Also, a former NBA coaches offered to connect me with a new Chrysler program – one that prepared qualified minorities to become owners of dealerships. My new "go-go" fired up attitude had me confident and ready to take the risk.

It was an era of transition and economic flux in the nation's inner cities and my role was to be the point person (manager of minority franchises) responsible for shutting down dealerships that were failing. Do this, I was told, and when the economic wheel upturns, I'd be early in line for my own dealership. But, minority dealerships were being offered in areas that white owners were evacuating; areas where credit was poor and the chance of success minimal. I didn't like or appreciate the situation. In another book, I will go into greater detail regarding Earl Lloyd's intelligence, friendship, inspiration, and what his mentoring meant to that stage of my career.

Meanwhile, Honeywell had been calling and this time it was the Vice Chairman who set forth a guarantee of executive training and advancement. There were eight different businesses operating under the Honeywell holding company structure worldwide and an opportunity for young executives to live in the progressive Minneapolis community or to live wherever they wanted in the world as careers developed.

Meanwhile, Honeywell sent me a plane ticket and I immediately flew back to a union that would prove to be durable, challenging and extremely rewarding. That's not to say it was as precise in development as had been promised. Several times supervisors found reasons for detours, but I was stubborn and had assurances that my evaluation would be based on performance. Aside from a few visual insensitivities and biases, every stop at Honeywell was a progressively greater learning platform.

Later in my career, serving on Boards of Directors was a breeze after the exposure and training I received at Honeywell. I went from human resources to marketing to factory management to business unit venture management and finally the lead worldwide corporate marketing officer sitting next to CEO, Mike Bonsignore. Mike was a good man who respected my opinions, gave me freedom, and watched my back as I did his.

In the early months of my Honeywell association, my progress was put on hold by a life-threatening development. During a Globetrotters' game years earlier, I was accidentally kicked in the side while on the floor. What I thought to be only broken ribs actually included bruised diaphragm. Side effects from that injury continued until a Labor Day weekend in St. Louis – the diaphragm ruptured, spilling bile and other waste into my chest cavity. A succession of hospitals and doctors were involved before proper surgery and antibiotics were determined. What a nightmare and wake-up call. All the work, all the preparation, and it was a life threatening illness that put me on the sidelines. It was like a light switch going out. But Honeywell continued my salary, paid all medical bills and stood beside me.

I spent 2 months in intensive care and at one point I thought I was drifting into the afterlife; at another point, word spread around that at age 29, I actually died. When corrective measures were finally implemented, I was down to less than 100 pounds. Six months elapsed and I returned to my job in Minneapolis, but it would be two years before my strength returned to normal.

Little did I know at the time how much this life threatening event would change everything in my life. The thoughts of ever palying competitive basketball were completely erased. The mystery of how much family meant and the love of friends was no longer a questions. I was totally crippled in mind and body. What was left was hope and the power of God-given determination. Long before I could walk around again, I'd spend hours thinking of the love of my Mom and Dad and neighbors in Edwardsville. It occurred to me very profoundly how critical one's health is how important relationships are to your existence. For example, no one from the University of Illinois showed up or called, no one from the Globetrotters showed up or wrote a note; even my good friend Gov Vaughn never called or sent a message. Lying there in bed, I discovered a comfortable spiritual space which even today I live in--in that hospital bed while draining gallons of abscess' and fluids from my chest, all I thought was how blessed my life had been and how much I wanted to show that I could achieve more and how much gratitude I wanted to share with the hundreds of people who had helped me along the way. I also became determined to navigate around all the barriers and obstacles I had come to use as excuses.

Meanwhile, progress through Honeywell's vast network at times was a sad reminder that the world was not yet under one roof. A talented management employee resigned because he didn't want to work for a person of color. I had to go to my boss and say, "We just lost one of our best people because of me."

Even more devastating was a moment involving a top senior assistant whom, I thought, also had become a close friend. I was at his home for a festive holiday dinner when one of his sons said, "I'm so glad that a nice man like Mr. Jackson works for my dad." As the reality of the comment sunk in, I was crushed with disbelief, I felt as though I was suffocating. Effusive apologies were offered but none could erase the fact that for two years, he'd been so embarrassed by the nature of our work association, that he couldn't reveal I was his boss to his family. He was a good man and I forgave him over a later dinner with his family. He apologized and we moved on – that kind of stupidity I consider a disease and should be pitied. The relentless, insidious, disruption of racial bias again was reinforced in my career.

My success is was becoming linked to an ability to step around obstacles, like a point guard moving toward the basket looking for a shot or an assist. My wife, Cathy says I am the most forgiving person she has ever known. My values are simple (F.O.R.), Forgiveness, Objectivity, and Resilience (get over it). I am able to push through most obstacles and continue forward. I think my willingness to do so, and also to catalogue them for high-level discussions of behavioral practices, helped to alter the culture at Honeywell and the Globetrotters. Even today, I practice seeing events as I want them to be and not as they are, accepting with faith that life and human interactions are imperfect "works in progress."

As I advanced to a salary and benefits situation that made our lives more than comfortable, I was also investing and making entrepreneurial moves designed to increase my future income potential. It was clear to me that the corporate retirement plan, social security, and 401k's wouldn't satisfy my economic needs after I left the corporate world. I understood early that I wanted more and I wanted to give more. I want my kids "to have the gold" and a fair start in life to carry on the legacy of my grandfathers and their families.

When I decided to step aside as a Honeywell Senior Vice-President, I was proud to be one of the company's senior officers and one of eight on its corporate policy committee. At that time, only four people reported directed to the CEO and I was one of them. When I looked back over 20 years and where I started, it was a remarkable achievement, a stressful and demanding journey. I loved every stop along the way. Who would ever dream or guess that my background would result in a career that my Dad refers to with pride as an improbable long shot?

When I decided to step aside as a Honeywell Senior Vice-President, I was proud to be one of the company's senior officers and one of eight on its corporate policy committee. At that time, four people reported directly to the CEO and I was one of them. Overall in 1994 we had come a long way, but it's the next generation that will take the final stride. Like basketball two decades earlier, my window of opportunity passed – even though my desires and dreams hadn't.

Still, it had become obvious the final step up the Fortune 500 corporate ladder would not be available to Mannie Jackson. In discussions with other top black executives, I've learned that Honeywell was no different than most other major corporations in that regard. We were proud to watch Xerox, American Express, and few companies make the case for non-white and no-male leadership. Overall we had come a long way, but it's the next generation that will take the final stride. Like basketball two decades earlier, my window of opportunity for leadership in corporate America passed, even though my desires and dreams hadn't.

I methodically loosened my association with Honeywell after a run as President and General Manager of two successful ventures. I did this to indulge my independent entrepreneurial whims and begin a new phase in my life. I started this book 16 years ago and every few months a new chapter and opportunities unfold. There has been much preparation in my life and in your playbook leading up to this point. It's my plan to share with you the story of how a very common and ordinary worker goes about actualizing dreams. Please come with me to **Step 7**, to *Publish Your Dream Plan Book*, and become the author of your dreams.

Step 7: Publish Your Dream Plan Book

Concept Practiced: Connect with the Thinking Stuff

This is where the rubber meets the road—actually where the pen meets the paper…wait, no… where the author meets software!

Bring your dream statement, dream elements, dream theme, and dream script together to input and upload them using BOOK SMART.

In a few moments you will click the publish button; and in a few days you will receive your **Dream Plan Book** via ground shipping.

*You are going to ignite the thinking stuff with your published **Dream Plan Book**.*

The purpose of this step is to build and publish your **Dream Plan Book.** You have composed your dream statement, collected dream elements, and written your dream script. These will be typed into your **dream plan book** from your playbook notes into the BOOK SMART software.

You may have a very simple, short dream that only requires a couple of pages of photos, and a couple of pages of writing.

The first one you may consider an trial or a sample, it does not have to be perfect! You may go back and create another storybook on another subject, at a later time. You can improve upon this one, make it longer, and add details and even more illustrations later. You can simply purchase another ***Dream Plan Book*** and will not need to purchase this entire course again!

If you haven't done so already, download the BOOK SMART software to your computer. Next you will create a title for your new ***Dream Plan Book*** to become author of your dreams!

PLAY 7-1: Title It

Concept Practiced: *Connect with the Thinking Stuff*

PLAY 7-1: Remembering how powerful words are, list keywords, theme words, and emotional words that describe the heart and action of your dream:

1 _____
2 _____
3 _____
4 _____
5 _____

List unique qualities and special details that you will bring to your dream story:

1 _____
2 _____
3 _____
4 _____
5 _____

Keeping in mind your true dream objective, (why you want money, why you want to meet the love of your life, etc.) write a title that sums up the big picture of your story. Remember how powerful it is to write in the present tense. *This title will be inputted when you create the new file for your* **Dream Plan Book.**

Title of my *Dream Plan Book*

> **SAMPLE PLAY 7-1**
>
> Title of My Dream Plan Book:
> *100 Days to My Most Fit Body Building Beauty*

My Dream Plan Book Title:_____

_____
_____
_____
_____

PLAY 7-2: Input It!

Concept Practiced: *Connect with the Thinking Stuff*

PLAY 7-2: You are almost ready to click on the "order book" button.

Use the title you created in the previous play to name your new book project in the BOOK SMART software.

Your dream statement, dream elements, and dream script are the basis for your storyline. These are located in PLAY 3-3, 4-3, 5-3; and you may type these into the text area of the book started in your BOOK SMART software.

Next, upload your graphics, to include the dream elements that you have collected. For example, if your ***Dream Plan Book*** has become your itinerary to Italy, then upload photos of Italian art, the poetry you have collected, and your maps, and travel schedule, day by day.

The "get photo" button at the top allows you to browse directly from your computer. Photos and graphics will need to be in a 300 dpi jpg format. If not, it may come out fuzzy or pixilated, but that isn't necessarily the end of the world. This book is for you; it's not going to be professionally marketed for the whole world to see!

My ***Dream Plan Book*** "100 days to my most Fit Body Building Beauty" has its focus on strength training. I uploaded key weight training exercises, as well as a "before photo." I created a file folder in my computer for photos and graphics to be uploaded to my ***Dream Plan Book!***

The "page view" feature allows you to preview your book in various layout forms. You may click on edit if you want to move things around, edit your words, type style, add frames or borders; or change the style of the layout, Click on the preview button at the bottom of the screen to see how it will look in its final form.

SAMPLE PLAY 7-2

Input it:
I type in my dream statement, dream theme, and dream script from my workbook, into the text areas of my book.

Upload it:
I uploaded photos and graphics from my computer, which I have been collecting in a file.

Upload it:
Cover photographs and back over graphics or illustrations.

☐ Input Text

☐ Upload Images

☐ Upload Cover

PLAY 7-3: Publish It!

Concept Practiced: *Connect with the Thinking Stuff*

PLAY 7-3: Before you click on the button in the bottom right hand corner of BOOK SMART software that says "order book," it is advisable to print out a preview copy.

Preview your ***Dream Plan Book*** using the "preview" button on the bottom right of the page. Look for obvious spelling errors, misplaced graphics, spacing issues, and layout

Before you click print, which is in top left FILE menu, be sure the paper size is set properly. Select a custom size, rather than the normal 8.5 x 11 paper. Type in 7" x 7" for paper size within the printer set up box.

Once you print your pre-production book, you now may proofread it. If you are not too anxious, give it a day or two to sit, before you actually click on the "order book" button at the far right bottom of the BOOK SMART software. You might get some additional inspirational to add some nice finishing touches.

When ready to publish, click on the "order book" button, and you will be asked for your password and login name. Once you provide that, your book will be uploaded to the publishing site. Then go to check out, make payment, and your shipping address!

At the end of this workbook, you may follow a detailed step-by-step dream plan book tutorial.

Once you have published your dream plan book, you will receive notification via e-mail, when your book ships, and it will include a tracking number. Wait for your published ***Dream Plan Book*** to arrive by ground shipping. Congratulations, You are now **AUTHOR OF YOUR DREAMS!**

SAMPLE PLAY 7-3

I will print out a copy of my Dream Plan Book before publishing so that I may proofread it. I can still rearrange the graphic components and text before clicking on the ORDER BOOK button.

☐ Proof copy is printed out

☐ Changes are marked on the proof copy

☐ Changes are made in the BookSmart File

☐ Dream Plan Book is ordered

Chapter 8:
Professional Basketball Action

NBA ACTION

> One day while I was still at Honeywell, I received an intriguing phone call from Esquinas in San Diego. He announced, "Let's you and I bring NBA basketball back to San Diego!" Little did I know...that was the start of a new dream for me to become our country's first African-American owner of a prominent basketball team!

In the early 1990's, my friend Richard Esquinas enjoyed a brief but stunning spin through the national media due to a book he'd written, one which detailed a series of golf matches with NBA superstar Michael Jordan. In the book, Esquinas claimed to have won more than $1 million from personal bets with Jordan on those matches.

I can't authenticate Esquinas's material, but I do know that they met and played. I played in several of the games which quickly got too rich and too pressure-packed for my "weekend" game and 6 handicap. I have to say, however, I've never had as much fun or enjoyed the game more with anyone before or since. As I recall, Jordan was a super competitor and Esquinas's game kept getting stronger and stronger.

Then, because of our golfing connections, in 1989 a group of NBA players, including Jordan, staged an exhibition charity game in San Diego. Most attended a party at the home of Harry Cooper, who is the uncle of Esquinas' wife Kerry. It was around that time, Michael met Richard Esquinas.

San Diego was a vacation destination for my family and I had met Esquinas several years earlier on a golf course at Coronado Island. We developed a friendship that ultimately diverted into a business relationship.

A pioneer in computer research, Harry Cooper, Esquinas's uncle-in-law, made a small fortune from real estate gains and a company he had formed and sold. Following his marriage to Kerry Cooper, Harry's niece, Esquinas became an associate in one of Cooper's enterprises.

I liked the fact that Esquinas was knowledgeable sports fanatic. He wanted to build working relationships in that field and eventually persuaded Cooper that it would be feasible to build a new, state of the art arena on the land Cooper owned in the Sorrento Valley area northwest of San Diego. He also convinced Cooper that a minority ownership team would have a competitive advantage. As a result, one day while I was still at Honeywell, I received an intriguing phone call from Esquinas in San Diego. He announced, "Let's you and I bring NBA basketball back to San Diego!" Little did I know...that was the start of a new dream for me to become our country's first African-American owner of a prominent basketball team!

For the arena building project to succeed an anchor tenant would be required, meaning an NBA team would need to be its primary tenant. Esquinas was asking me to be an investor. However, from the beginning I was uneasy with Harry Cooper; and so when we finally reached an agreement it was based on a simple stipulation.

My stipulation was that we were to be in the sports business only. And as owner of an NBA San Diego Franchise, my team would be the arena's primary tenant. It became my responsibility to lead the group to acquire, finance, and manage an NBA team with the "Cooper Arena" as its home base. I wanted no part of building or financing of the arena. The other part of my stipulation was they would agree to stay out of the basketball part of it. So we reached a partnership agreement and I soon put together an impressive alignment of wealthy and influential sports investors to form the San Diego NBA team.

We then did an exhaustive research on the San Diego market for how to build a first class professional basketball team to exceed the standards of the NBA. Twice the NBA had been in San Diego; and twice it had left. Sadly, the nature of the second parting left the NBA and its promoters with a black eye and I was told there was sentiment to refuse San Diego another chance to host an NBA team.

We learned that San Diego's last NBA bid, the Clippers, purchased in 1981 by Donald T. Sterling who was a Los Angeles real estate Tycoon who promised to spare no expense in creating an instant winner. Instead, Sterling soon was downsizing staff and payroll. With predictable results, attendance declined, and the team ultimately failed in San Diego and was moved up to the Los Angeles Sports Arena in 1984.

More research showed that fans in San Diego felt the problem may have been with team leadership and not NBA basketball. There were strong indications that perhaps with a glistening new arena, professional leadership, and a solid marketing plan, success could be assured.

We all know however, that business and matters of life are often more complex. I wanted our start-up to look and feel like the Phoenix Suns, and the Portland Trailblazers. I began to think branding and building trust, which is what was needed most in this San Diego market. I knew that we must start from "day one," to build trust.

Then in June of 1989, with much media fanfare I was introduced as the leader of an ownership group committed to bringing NBA basketball back to San Diego. Early response was promising. A season ticket campaign gathered steam and everywhere I appeared publically there was fan excitement and momentum. Esquinas did an excellent job promoting new ownership and creating excitement for an NBA basketball team in San Diego. The theme song for our campaign was Patti's Labelle's song, "New Attitude."

Quickly as momentum was building, it all began to unravel. Working against our success were two forces that as they collided, became overwhelming. One force was that the City of San Diego would not get on board to support our new NBA team, and the other force was thought to be our association with Harry Cooper.

Esquinas was a smart and hard working marketer. But at times gave the impression that he was more interested in the visibility, celebrity, and golf games with Jordan. Harry was more businesslike, but he too, seemed intoxicated by the publicity. The San Diego establishment was very conservative, and even Jack Kemp, Secretary of H.U.D. who was enlisted to our cause, couldn't shake off the negative labels assumed by our association with Harry Cooper.

The Clippers/Sonics Exhibition game was the deathblow on my dream to bring an NBA team to San Diego. By then, Cooper's celebrity had attracted the chummy attention of Donald Sterling, now L.A. Clippers owner, who had been inviting Cooper to parties at Sterling's beachfront spread in Malibu; and they could be seen embracing at courtside prior to the exhibition game. Sterling was the last San Diego NBA owner who had "kidnapped" the Clippers to L.A. and a possible "funny business" association between Sterling and Cooper's new bid for San Diego NBA arena could not be ignored.

At a time when our group had been attempting to make an honest presentation for an arena/NBA partnership with Cooper/Esquinas, the high profile Cooper/Sterling alliance was devastating both in terms of publicity and trust. Watching Cooper and Sterling embrace at courtside in a city where Sterling was viewed with some contempt, was the punctuation mark on a dying business relationship, and final evaporation of my dream to own an NBA Team.

Our team quickly disengaged and left a dead project in the hands of Cooper and Esquinas, but only after a loss of a substantial financial investment. It was an expensive lesson, but an important one. As I look back, every obstacle and barrier could have been managed with more time and better leadership. In the Epilogue of this book, I talk about opportunity evaluation in terms of real, win, and worth. No matter how many sound business principles are involved, the most important factors are the choice of associates--ones with unequivocal passion and focus.

And lastly, a dream in the making which seems to stall does not need to die, but only to navigate a curve in the road where it can find fresh new action and direction.

HARLEM GLOBETROTTERS ACTION

Two years after I played my final game as a Harlem Globetrotter, founder and owner Abe Saperstein died. Abe left no will. The team was his family's biggest asset. The Globetrotters consequently went into probate as the largest portion of his estate.

In liquidating his assets, I am told by reliable sources, the court placed a $3 million value on the team, a substantial sum for a sports franchise in 1969. Metromedia, whose mission was to grow the Globetrotters' audience as a youth-oriented comedic property by way of a television cartoon, eventually acquired the team. I was shocked and hurt that one of the greatest teams ever and most well known global ambassadors would exit the sports scene as cartoon characters. To this day, I can recite the superstars who built the championship Globetrotters and the legacy of a great franchise.

The imagination finds it easy to visualize the unintended consequences of segregation – where great lawyers, scientists, musicians, artists, photographers, educators, entrepreneurs and sports stars are relegated to 3rd class citizens and kicked shamelessly out of the mainstream of free enterprise and democracy because of the color of their skin and resulting from greed and immorality of the policy makers. Imagine the Globetrotters today if the NBA continued its segregated way – the 20 best black players in the world would be divided up between the NY Tens and Chicago's Harlem Globetrotters. Imagine Kobe, LeBron, Wade, Pierce, Shaq, on the same teams?

Rev. Jesse Jackson, Sr. in 2002 said, "Had the NBA and colleges remained segregated we may have never known how great the game of basketball could become." Introduced the game of basketball to millions around the world, The Harlem Globetrotters put the game in its most favorable light.

Many baby-boomers, now in the 45-60 demographic, learned of the Globetrotters through that television cartoon series. While the cartoon and later a CBS television series proved popular, the negative of the venture was it trivialized the team's legacy of their Hall of Fame play on the court. Ownership eventually passed to the International Broadcast Company (IBC), a Minneapolis-based entertainment group that also had under its broad umbrella, amusement parks, live theaters and the Ice Capades. The company borrowed heavily during the 1980's and the Globetrotters became its cash cow. The team never missed a touring season, but by the time IBC went into Chapter 11 in 1991, the financial drain had caused a significant decline in the Harlem Globetrotter product and image.

Many black people my dad's age were saddened and felt betrayed by the team's constant clowning and antics and who they had become. My family would say to me, "Why are you wasting your time?" For me it was my dream driven by an aspiration to restore the proud legacy of a champion with a heart. It was the dreamer and insider, who learned from the team's creator what its mission was to be. It was me; a former player who understood the pinnacle of excellence this team had like no other in sports had reached.

The talent level slipped to a point where the players were a parody of themselves and the quality of the players values involved had also plunged. IBC was so indifferent to the Globetrotters' proud history that they even persuaded Meadowlark Lemon – arguably one of the most famous Globetrotters of all time, who had retired 15 years earlier – to stage a comeback. This was done, not for the benefit of youngsters who had never seen him play, but to appease a bankruptcy creditor. During Meadowlark's tour, which lasted 55 games, he frequently contacted me to lament the organization's decay. I never blame IBC for the mess left behind by Metromedia. In my view, bankruptcy was inevitable when the brand drifted from its core competency and relevance. The team's act had become stale and out-dated.

During that period I was investigating the possibility of buying the team. I had been thinking about paybacks for the successes life had provided me and it seemed that a wonderful contribution would be to take an African-American institution of such historical significance, revitalize it and make certain it would have a future of financial health and positive influence.

More so I thought of closing the doors, doing a movie, writing a book, and setting up a museum to sell merchandise. The Globetrotters under Saperstein created and innovated so much that is now forgotten. When the NBA struggled, the "Trotters" stepped up to help the NBA teams survive and draw crowds. Today no one acknowledges this or the many other Trotter global innovations. Some today debate--who was the better black team, the New York Tens or the Harlem Globetrotters. Frankly, who cares. They were both great teams, and maybe the best, but more importantly, they were both products of a segregated society.

Research confirmed that the Globetrotters' infrastructure had fallen apart. Through my NBA bid, I had learned enough about sports economics to be confident that, if retooled and properly marketed, the Globetrotters could again be a viable, popular entry in the sports and entertainment world. I now knew there were television and sports arenas all over the world looking for branded content.

For 12 years I learned two things; great stories attract people and comedy built around victims and underdogs can be the basis of endless humor. The big surprise in the Globetrotters case teases its audience with questions: A) who are these people, B) how good are they? and C) in the right setting, laughter is a universal language. These three factors put in motion create compelling theater, drama, and entertainment. We would give the world better basketball than anyone imagined, (the art of over delivering), and better people than anyone else in our industry. And finally, we were in the business of creating memories and dreams.

The first purchase price I was quoted was $44 million, which I thought was too high. Over a period of time though, we put together a committed partnership and through a series of intricate negotiations were able to acquire 80 percent ownership of the Globetrotters for $5.5 million. I was the majority owner and totally responsible for the team's reorganization and resurgence after investing over one million dollars.

I knew the plan could not be activated without great, dedicated people like Tex Harrison, Colleen Lenihan, Chad Groth, Mike Wilson, Lou Dunbar, Mike Syracuse and Jeff Munn. Colleen was a brilliant 21-year old pre-med student who dropped everything in her life to support the dream of reviving the Globetrotters. She was the human computer who started everyday with the goal of pushing me and the organization to its limits. She has no formal business training, but she was smart, focused, and dedicated to the organization's goals. She, Chad, Jeff, and Mike Syracuse were the nucleus of my management dream team. Others tried, but fell to the side under the pressure and demands needed to get the "ball rolling."

Our story drove hard to pose the questions that created curiosity and sampling. The first of which was, Who is this up-start former player who wants to fix this broken down wagon of yesteryear? and How could he expect to bring those clowning routines into balance with the skills of the NBA, NCAA, and streetball (hop hop style)?

And so after 5 years of performances by Mike Wilson, competitive college tours, Vegas style magic shows, Burger King sponsored documentary, FUBU (For Us By Us)sponsored apparel accepted by entertainers, fundraisers on four continents and South America, and with Hall of Fame recognition, the tipping point was reached for the The Harlem Globetrotters to be known and loved the world over.

Believing so wholeheartedly in this unlikely dream, I positioned reluctant investors so they would receive a 15% annual interest coupon over three years guaranteed! Dennis Mathisen and I personally secured this promise. Between the two of us, we owned 85% of 80% of the team. However, I had the option to cash everyone out including the bank for a multiple of EBITA. EBITA was multiplied by 12 and the cash was divided by the number of investors and the pot of gold distributed by shares held. That's a brief simplistic description to demonstrate the confidence I had in turning the profit and growth curves around. The payments ranged from 600K to 13M – well worth it for me to be alone going into a risky future and to reward my friends early. The bank asked for a similar deal on the 4.5 million dollar purchase loan.

By the hour that acquisition closed, I discovered that Dirk Post, my advocate in the bank was right by insisting that we have a failsafe operating plan. Even though our goal was leadership in sports entertainment, we didn't publicize ourselves to the sports pages – I went to the financial writers. Publications like *The Bloomsberg, The Wall Street Journal, NY Times,* and *USA Today* responded with thoughtful, well researched presentations about the business and marketing abilities of the Globetrotters' under new management. This was a big risk, but vital for attracting future corporate partners through an objective and positive "slant" on the business upside possibilities. This message was hoped to influence our owners as we negotiated contracts and sports stories.

The team's two-week training camp included business classes on what is expected from a new Globetrotter. This included how they were to deal with the public, money management and how to conduct themselves as role models; how they were players and marketing representatives of an African-American institution and how to be mentally wired to be positive influences in communities across the country and around the world. We wanted to become the ultimate brand and content provider– using the same principles given to me by Abe Saperstein years earlier - great basketball ambassadors of goodwill and family entertainment (not buffoons or clowns).

Players had to understand that no one becomes a Globetrotter overnight. To learn the ball-handling techniques and skills unique to our style and be able to perform them in the flow of a game takes at least two years to master. Whether you're talking about a Marquez Hayner, "Goose" Tatum, Connie Hawkins, Sonny Boswell, "Showboat" Hall, Meadowlark Lemon, Hallie Bryant, you're talking about Hall of Famers and movement of a basketball that causes great athletes and fans to say, *How are they doing that?* When Magic Johnson's agent Lon Rosen and I spoke on the phone to discuss Magic joining the Globetrotters – perhaps playing a few games I had to tell him, "We are scheduled to play 9 NBA first round draft picks and we need Magic badly, but Magic can't just show up and play for the Globetrotters."

That's because Magic would need to spend more time training than he could imagine to actually fit within the unit. My favorite NBA player of all time happens to be "Magic" Johnson. He gets it. He's expertly talented and he always leads his team to victory. He's a considerate "feel good guy" who remembers and connects with the souls of people he meets. He doesn't just play the game – he is the game. My thanks to him for all the love and support he gave the Harlem Globetrotters and me.

Ten non-players stand out in my 13-year ownership – Mike Syracuse, Jeff Munn, Colleen Lenihan (Olsen), Chad Groth, Chris Clouser, Dennis Mathisen, Paul Fireman, Ed Garvey, Linda Netjes and Oprah Winfrey.

Each of them will be a full chapter in my next book. None of the growth, success, and legacy of 1992 – 2005 would have been possible without Dennis Mathisen's unique and positive friendship – he always supported me and the organization unconditionally.

It is hard for me to fathom the number of presentations I gave for loans, investments, and sponsors. While I never lost my confidence, I was shocked when there was a time that I couldn't seem to raise as little as 5K from friends and business associates. Everything turned around one day when a friend who worked at Northwest Airlines asked me to tell him about what I was doing. "This is great organization and I believe in you and your plans. Northwest will take a sponsorship plus cover travel, along with advertising to cover a significant share." He walked me into the Board of Directors meeting and we sealed the deal. I was both shocked and deeply grateful. Not long after that, just two years into my Globetrotter ownership, we received a purchase offer of $30 million showing we were on the right track (not bad for an original $5.5 million purchase price). Offers we would receive 10 years later helped our biggest dreams for the Harlem Globetrotter to be realized.

MY DREAM TEAM IN ACTION

When I purchased the Harlem Globetrotters in 1993, I became the first African-American to own a major sports team. My goal was to make the Globetrotters a powerful championship basketball team to entertain and motivate young people while giving to charities around the world. One of the ways to accomplish this was to put people in touch with the legacy of this great American institution. Recently, this goal came alive with our 77th season theme, "Reclaiming the Game...Old School Fun with New Flavor." This theme refects the idea the Globetrotters will return to their roots of entertaining, as well as "taking on all challengers, to reclaim the global leadership as ambassadors of goodwill.

In 2003, the team had tripled in size in 10 years and was the buzz throughout the NBA after having recruited serveral of its popular players, credit given to Gene Keady of Purdue. Tom Izzon of Michigan State and St. John University. The team was also in demand from Divison 1 college coaches and were playing a half dozen nationally televised games against those top ranked teams. We were rolling at a record pace while remembering all the chosen charities as lead donors; hip-hop musical artists and high profile youth and adults could be seen wearing Globetrotter apparel on televisions and at sports events.

Then an award winning documentary played worldwide for two months, and Burger King, a team sponsor ran content driven television commercials after the team's 2002 Hall of Fame Enshrinement. A new flavor was also evident in the payers game attire, which was designed by FUBU as a result of a licensing partnership. FUBU, experienced a brisk sale of $40 million in retail sales the first two years of sponsorship in 5,000 locations worldwide. By the 10th year, the team had over 20 top sponsors spending over $75 million to help in the promotion of the team. In 1996, the Globetrotters finished second place in the LA Summer Pro League during the NBA player lock out. Everyone involved in the business of basketball attended those games. With this kind of visibility, our chief scout Chad Groth was able put an excellent team together lead by Wun Versher and Reggie Phillips.

Then in 1999, 2000, and 2002 "Q" ratings were showing further evidence of the Globetrotters popularity, particularly in the African-American Community. According to the 2002 "Q" Ratings, African-Americans were nearly twice as likely to be familiar with the Harlem Globetrotters and three times as likely to choose the Globetrotters as one of their favorites. Overall the Globetrotters ranked second to Michael Jordan and ahead of Tiger Woods and in the top two percent of all 1700 "Q" performers in 2003 and 2004!

With that, The Harlem Globetrotters' popularity had become fact and was sealed. No team and few leagues annually drew as many spectators as The Globetrotters. According to the Naismith Basketball Hall of Fame, no team has given as much to sports as these African-American Ambassadors. Bob Ryan of the *Boston Globe* wrote, "The Globetrotters have outlived the depression, two world wars, rock n' roll, disco, and just about every "pop" phenomenon imaginable over the past 70 years. Whether you live in Bangkok, or Boston, if you haven't seen and admired the team's achievements on and off the court, you can count yourself in a very small minority."

We were single minded in our purpose to restore the relevance and the innovative leadership of the Abe Saperstein era and fill a void in championship play and entertainment only possible with a global team. Our management team took on the challenge, and by 2005 we were taking on the Olympic Champion Argentina team for a $1 million world championship prize in Florida. The Globetrotters were no joke, no longer impotent cartoon characters! The team had the highest jumper in basketball, world record holder Mike Wilson.

As for the most outstanding highlights and memories, in early 2000, we were guests of Prince Charles in England promoting charity, health, and diversity in entrepreneurship. We visited 20 bank conferences in 2 days. The team was hosted in 1994-1995 by Nelson Mandela and Engen Petroleum in South Africa and made an appearance with Pope John Paul II before 85,000 onlookers at the Vatican. And as many times before after these moments, I had to pinch myself, wondering if I was literally dreaming while realizing that my dream to own a basketball team had actually come true!

How did these boardroom sized dreams of an Illmo, Missouri, boy born in a boxcar move from fantasy to reality? Walk over with me to the next dream step where you will learn about how to receive your dream with action with **Step 8**, *Inspire Your Dream with Action*.

Step 8:
Inspire Your Dream With Action

Concept Practiced: *Power of the Present Moment*

"THE DREAM: To see it in the distance is but the first step; to go the distance requires taking the rest of the steps."

Read, review, and recite your Dream Plan Book daily—be inspired to take action steps that bring you closer to the realization of your dream.

We talk about steps because making your dreams come true on purpose involves a series of steps. The *Dreams to Reality* Action Plan has endeavored to gently walk you through these 10 steps to dream success!

In the first seven steps of the dreams to reality process, we have guided you to position yourself to envision your dream! In step seven, together we have brought you to the brink of your dreams by enabling you publish your *Dream Plan Book*. Once you receive your *Dream Plan Book* from the shipper you will have be best possible vision of your dream. The purpose of this step is to practice the power and forms of action to speed the receiving of your dream.

PLAY 8-1: Meditation Action

Concept Practiced: *Power of the Present Moment*

PLAY 8-1: When your *Dream Plan Book* arrives, set aside five powerful minutes each morning and evening for meditation on your book.

This will help you to focus and envision your dream; stimulate thoughts and energy required to create the dream momentum to bring your dream into reality.

List additional action steps you are inspired to take when reading, reviewing, and meditating on, your ***Dream Plan Book.***

> **SAMPLE PLAY 8-1**
>
> *After reviewing my Dream Plan Book, which outlines my 100 days body-building plan, I am inspired to add another layer of strength training to my workout routine.*

1 _____

2 _____

3 _____

PLAY 8-2: Now Action

Concept Practiced: *Power of the Present Moment*

PLAY 8-2: Sometimes our dream seems dim and far away, and we may become discouraged. But NOW is the most powerful moment we have. We can only act in the present moment. List things you can do NOW, each and every day that will bring your dream closer to you everyday. If you use NOW wisely, time is on your side!

> **SAMPLE PLAY 8-2**
>
> *When I look at these photos of Italian Art, and outdoor café…I can hear the birds, smell the fresh Espresso, gaze up at the amazing skies; and I can almost feel the warm fresh breeze of the Mediterranean Sea. I am inspired to take action and today I will take action steps to see my dream come true. I will get a book at the Library on how to speak Italian, write my cousin in Italy; and join the Italian Meetup group here in town.*

1 _____

2 _____

3 _____

4 _____

5 _____

PLAY 8-2: Now Action (Cont.)

Concept Practiced: *Power of the Present Moment*

PLAY 8-2: Speak and think of your dream as if already here. List feelings, thoughts, and visions that come to you when you think of your dream as being RIGHT NOW. Infuse your thoughts with the reality of how your dreams feels, and thinks, and looks like right now. Actions I want to take to give my dream the power of "nowness!"

1. _____

2. _____

3. _____

4. _____

5. _____

6. _____

7. _____

PLAY 8-3: Proactive Action

Concept Practiced: *Power of the Present Moment*

PLAY 8-3: This play is exciting, and risky. It involves applying extreme faith to the present moment. These are actions you take that may catapult you into your dream. When we planned our trip to Europe, we did not have the extra money, and did not know how we were going to do it.

We moved quickly into manifesting the dream because we took a proactive leap of faith. We selected a date, and bought airplane tickets. This was six months in advance. Over the next six months, a trade covered our accommodations, and then all we had left to do was come up with spending money!

Once you make a proactive move, you become invested in the dream, and the dream becomes energized.

List below proactive steps you may take to bring your dream into your present moment!

Warning: These proactive leaps of faith can be risky, and we do not advise doing these unless your faith is strong. Be prepared to move forward with no second-guessing, regrets, or guilt. These states of mind may pull you even further away from your dream than this action will take you. Be sure your faith is in place.

SAMPLE PLAY 8-3

Now that I have completely outlined my Itinerary to Italy, it is obvious that I will need to buy a train pass. If I buy it ahead of time, it's about half price-- that will be a proactive move projecting me into a commitment to take the trip!

Things I can do to draw my dream from the future into my present.

Chapter 9:
That Family Blessing We are Grateful

> Even the strongest of families has its unity challenged at some point. The ability to successfully deal with this adversity is what makes a strong family so special and provides its progeny with a superior chance to succeed.

Beginning in that boxcar in Illmo, Missouri, so many years ago, family and relationships provided a sinew that is as much, or more, responsible for my survival and success than any other factor.

Even the strongest of families has it unity challenged at some point. The ability to successfully deal with this adversity is what makes a strong family so special and provides its progeny with a superior chance to succeed. Most families come apart when they become too critical and judgmental and their intolerance erodes to hostility. Once you learn to tolerate, forgive and get over family flaws – the support given far outweighs the flaws. I'm blessed and I truly appreciate every member of my family- from Cathy ,Candy, Cassie, Randall, my very great sister Parge, my Dad, my brother Steve, Uncle Bob, Rhonda, my super-star and brilliant Aunt Dee, Nephew Bronson Mannie, my surrogate brother Gov, and others too many to mention who contributed to my Dreams and my wonderful story. I love you all.

As I close the last chapter of this book I receive news that my dad has a serious illness and my sister Marjorie and I placed our dad in Hospice care. We're in shock and we know the next several months will be the most difficult of our lives. My 92-year-old father Emmett is as upbeat as ever and continues to be a solid, rock-of-the-earth of person who is loved and respected by everyone. Our relationship today is stronger than ever because of values like forgiveness, objectivity and resilience. He's my dad and he can be odd and obsessive from time to time, but our job is to love him unconditionally. Being a great Dad doesn't mean being perfect; it means to me he cares in ways unique to him. I love him and I love his uniqueness and sometime onery and quirky ways.

My mother gave us her very best and dreamed the best for us. Our victories and achievements are her legacy and the fulfillment of her dreams.

I was returning from a Honeywell assignment to Florida when I met my wife-to-be Cathy Roberts. She was in Minneapolis to interview for a position with the Airlines, and this was before she received her MBA from Suffolk University. We shared a long and somewhat confrontational discussion about race relations, Affirmative Action, marketing, economics, and planning.

She was attractive, lively, very bright and down-to-earth. I had platonic friendships with a number of women and that same kind of friendship quickly developed between Cathy and myself from the first meeting. For months thereafter, we talked by telephone.

Later, as the friendship deepened, we finally addressed the fact that I was African-American and she was white. We didn't spend a lot of time sorting it out, but we knew there would be strong family reactions. My family was a little concerned, but supportive from the start; her parents a bit overwhelmed, as in "What do we tell our friends?" "What will they think of us?" and "What about possible children?" These reactions hurt; particularly when her mother quizzed everyone with the question, "What did we do wrong?"

Racial differences are often overrated in relationships between two people. To begin with, the odds of finding a person with whom you are compatible is fairly low. But Cathy and I started as friends and knew how to treat one another respectfully. We also have similar common interests, besides our love for each other.

As for career, Cathy is an ideal corporate wife. If a customer or co-worker raised their eyebrows a bit when first seeing us together, I never noticed and they were soon talking positively about the intelligent, well-focused lady married to Mannie Jackson. Cathy makes friends easily and her demeanor attracts confidence and loyalty. I've never known anyone who bonded so completely in friendship. If the measure of a person is the level of friendship they can attain, then Cathy is a star role model.

The most bonding thing in any marriage is a decision to have children. We have enjoyed our relationship with my adopted son Randall and two great daughters, Candace and Cassandra, who have made us about as happy and proud as two people can be. Obviously since birth, they have existed in a privileged, integrated world. They too, have many friends who reflect both sides of their heritage. They were excellent students and graduated from top tier colleges – NYU, DePaul, and Colombia. Both are independent and happy.

Cathy and I long ago made a conscious decision to be open and candid about the racial aspect of their lives. We stressed the positive aspects of both sets of grandparents and attempted to give the girls reasons to be proud of both their backgrounds. When pressed about their racial identity, we are comfortable with the label and proud of our African-American lineage and the term mixed-race. We are also comfortable accepting that they are unique and blessed – African and Eastern European, a good mix of both. Along with my adopted son Randall, we enjoy the goodnesss of a great family.

For our part, Cathy and I are both socially and politically active. We are blessed to have given generously to our favorite charities and try to stay happy, productive, and positive. Our children are blessed with good health and great minds, with friends of all colors and backgrounds. Like most families, we bless our lives one day at a time. Our Candace recently married and I welcome Son-in-Law Connor to the family and look foward to grandchildren.

Step 9 of the Dreams to Reality Workbook is powerful, so do not skip this one. It will teach you to cultivate the gratitude factor, probably the most effective tool for giving life to your dream and taking it from believing it to receiving it. Now it's time to find out what blesses you the most and how to *Awaken Your Dream With Thanks* – **Step 9!**

Step 9: *Awaken Your Dream With Thanks*

Concept Practiced: *Attraction Action of Gratitude*

Many books have been written, and documentaries made regarding the "law of attraction." The concept is that you attract events, people, and situations into your life, through the power of thought. If this is true, then the ultimate law of attraction is the Action of Gratitude!

If you take away ONE concept from this series, let it be this step, because gratitude is the most effective step in the entire **Dreams to Reality Process**.

The purpose of Step 9 is practice thanks in order to magnetize your dream towards you! The "attitude of gratitude" is more than being polite, creating small talk of your blessings, or acting happy and positive. The "action of gratitude" is powerful. It is the idea that you are continuously connected with your source, thankful for every dream has come true, every dream that is going to come true, and for those dreams that you are living right now.

True gratitude is so powerful that if you were to practice gratitude every day in every way, your life would be a total dream come true. The "on-purpose" action of gratitude accomplishes so many of the dream steps. It brings you closer to your source continuously, it keeps your thoughts focused on high energy, and it takes your thoughts away from the things that you don't want.

PLAY 9-1: Now Thanks

Concept Practiced: *Attraction Action of Gratitude*

PLAY 9-1: List the dreams that have come true and that you are living right now.

> **SAMPLE PLAY 9-1**
>
> *I am living the life of my dreams right now; I have the career of my dreams! I am working on the body of my dreams, and home of my dreams but I am truly thankful for the career of my dreams!*

Dreams that have come true already:

1. _____

2. _____

3. _____

4. _____

5. _____

PLAY 9-2: Daily Thanks

Concept Practiced: *Attraction Action of Gratitude*

PLAY 9-2: This is the most powerful play in this playbook! Simply make a list of the 10 things, people, or situations for which you are thankful every single day.

When I first started practicing this play, I sat down at my computer every morning and made a list of Ten Thankful Things. I printed out the list and posted them in my office! Now upon waking, I make the list in my mind, it became a powerful habit.

> **SAMPLE PLAY 9-2**
>
> *I wake up each morning and say my thanksgiving prayers daily.*

List 10 Things for which you are thankful:

1. _____

2. _____

3. _____

4. _____

5. _____

6. _____

7 _____

8 _____

9 _____

10 _____

More Thanks

_____
_____
_____
_____
_____
_____
_____
_____
_____
_____
_____
_____
_____
_____
_____
_____
_____

PLAY 9-3: Proactive Thanks

Concept Practiced: *Attraction Action of Gratitude*

PLAY 9-3: This play is similar to 9-2, except we are going to practice thankfulness for parts and pieces of the dream we are envisioning that is on its way. Because you are thanking ahead for what is to come, I have called it proactive thankfulness.

> **SAMPLE PLAY 9-3**
>
> *Each night before I go to bed, I read my Dream Plan Book and thank God for those dreams in the process of coming to me.*

Advanced thanks:

1 _____

2 _____

3 _____

4 _____

5 _____

6 _____

7 _____

8 _____

9 _____

10 _____

Personal Notes about Awakening My Dream With Thankfulness:

_____
_____
_____
_____
_____
_____
_____
_____
_____
_____
_____
_____
_____
_____
_____
_____
_____

FOURTH QUARTER: ACHIEVE

Mannie Jackson's Dream Planning Workbook

Chapter 10:
My Latest Greatest Dream

> *It is the last step; yet the beginning of a new way of life; walk with me one more step to Step 10, Become a Dream Achiever.*

When I think back to where my parents were in this country as young African-Americans during my adolescent and transition years compared to where I stand today, it seems there has been tremendous advancement in a relatively short time. That's true for some of us, but significant progress has been limited to numbers that are far too small. Because of that I fight feelings of isolation and guilt and frequently wonder – why me?

One vision of my future has me using whatever clout I've developed to help expand opportunities for others. I want to be a source for young men and women who hope to enter the economic, education and policy world. I want every child to find a Joe Lucco, John Watson, Dennis Mathisen, Bill Wray, Earl Lloyd or Ed Spencer to inspire and support them.

As more quality educational opportunities become available to young people who see me as a role model, it's vital to my legacy that I make my story and mentoring available. They need to understand the system from the inside and early. Our purpose is not to discourage young people from entering the adult world, but to bring perspective to their expectations and suggest methods of combating institutional roadblocks built into the infrastructure of democracy and capitalism as it exists today. I would want them to not personalize obstacles, but to remember everyone has something to overcome and by thinking strategically--the very issue seems to be a barrier often becomes assets and advantages. In my speeches I often share five example, regarding real case studies in business. My favorite one is the investment in the Harlem Globetrotters, which took a page out of Abe Saperstein's book.

For example, one should think of the corporate world as their training ground for developing a future private business. Along with many others, I did it and it worked for me.

Above all, one should not assume anything good will happen without risk without passion and hard work. If you hit walls in one geographic area, one company or field, don't be afraid to keep moving until you find one that's working. My good friend and Novellus

Corporation CEO, Richard "Rick" Hill said, "Find something to do that you are passionate about and a place to live that you care about and most importantly, get involved. Use your mind, your work and good intention to make you a better, happier, passionate person and leader."

A lesson learned from my experience in South Africa is that Americans somehow need to be educated to the fact that apartheid existed in this country and spend every day making sure as Nelson Mandela says, it never happens to anyone again.

We also need to do serious inventory of our own entrenched attitudes. European society, to which American style capitalism generally subscribes to and mistakenly operates under the notion that there must always be winners and losers. In the marketplace, that too often tends to apply to seller and customer. Reduced quality usually results from these adversarial situations and conflicting objectives. The best transactions are deals of equals and both sides respect the needs of the other and both sides are better off because of the relationship of respect in the transaction.

The African attitude is one studied and applied with extraordinary results by several nations, "Together, we can make this happen. And, when we do, we both win."

Enlightened companies in the United States are moving in this direction, but it's a strategy which needs to become widespread from all levels of society and not just top down – begin in your family, schools, and communities. Work with your friends, family, and co-workers to define winning.

This is all part of the diversity issue, one I hope to advance at every available opportunity. Women already have improved the workplace because they bring a different style and approach to accomplishing objectives. Likewise, people of Hispanic and African decent offer still another perspective. Don't reject that reality.

If the U.S. is to remain great in an increasingly competitive world and global society, we need to utilize and respect all human resources. Instead, the politics of segregation and prejudice cause us to focus so much on differences. In my opinion there is far too much liberal versus conservative ideology, greed and attitudes of winner takes all. We lose sight of the fact that otherwise, we're all pretty much the same. It shouldn't matter the religion, the race, or the sexual orientation. We want to contribute, we want respect, and we want our families to be safe. Most of all we occupy a planet that is shrinking and the space we occupy, and resources we demand need to be shared and utilized rationally if we are to survive as a species. There won't be a winner take all or dominant force in the future. There will be mutually beneficial beliefs and decisions shared by all who share the limited space on this planet.

My given name is Mannie Jackson and I was raised in a small rural midwestern part of the United States. I have been blessed and have been part of many wonderful experiences. I have seen many events and places on this planet, and have met scores of unusual and talented people. I am not sure how I started on this journey, but I have gone along for the ride in absolute amazement. I am honored to share my life and story in the hope that someone, somewhere will benefit and be positively influenced to keep moving forward in their dreams. My advise is to follow your own unique dream. I did...all the way from "boxcar to boardroom." And as Coach Lucco would say, "You gotta believe."

We end our dreams to reality journey in this workbook, with the learning to love and share the lifestyle of a dream achiever. It is the last step; yet the beginning of a new way of life; walk with me one more step to Step 10, *Become a Dream Achiever*.

Step 10: Become a Dream Achiever

Concept Practiced: *Live, Share, Expand Your Dream*

The most exciting thing about being a successful dream achiever, is sharing it with those we love. To experience a dream come true, without sharing it, is truly sad. Therefore, it is imperative we learn to live, share, and expand our dreams to include those we love, and to include our world. Now its time to learn to DREAM BIG!

At the beginning of this series, we asked you to start small to learn the skill set of dreams to reality. Small successes create confidence, and confidence creates more success, which builds dream momentum.

Once you learn the dreams steps and personalize them as yours, you may create big dreams. The purpose of this step is to encourage you to apply these steps again and again to dream big for your world!

At the time of this writing, Barack Obama has become the first African American President of the United States. I reflect on the larger dream that started playing on the American stage some 40 years ago. Martin Luther King had a dream. That dream was larger than Martin Luther, It was so big that it reached into our "now" and has affected all of mankind; having set the stage for Barack Obama, another big dreamer.

Strengthen your dream muscles and take dream achieving to the next level. Be as courageous as those who have gone before you, and don't forget to shoot for the moon—and the stars!

Share your dream successes online at www.AuthorYourDreams.com, and share your dreams with those who are supportive. Sharing your dream successes will give you the incentive to follow though.

PLAY 10-1: Now Dream Big

Concept Practiced: *Live, Share, Expand Your Dream*

> **SAMPLE PLAY 10-1**
>
> *Having identified my big dreams, I have plans to create another Dream Plan Book!*

PLAY 10-1: List Your Big Dreams

My big dreams to affect the world around me and my next dream plan books:

1. _____

2. _____

3. _____

4. _____

5. _____

Epilogue

Mannie's Words of Wisdom

A person's philosophy of how to conduct both their personal and business life obviously is shaped over a period of time. More than a decade after I joined Honeywell, I had clearly learned from some smart, successful, and caring leaders a list of personal differentiators that became my cornerstones; ones with which I am comfortable and consistent with in their application. I always begin by taking a deep breath and imagine that I am 30,000 feet above reality before I return to it. I get a better look at problems and possible outcomes. As we near the end of our *dreams to reality* journey, I share these philosophies with you here.

SHOWING UP

It was Woody Allen who said that 97 percent of success is created simply by showing up; and as told my Globetrotter players "being late is not an option." To me, in a more specific sense, showing up means meeting people and engaging yourself. This often requires sacrifice and discipline because in doing so, one often forfeits personal comfort and ideology conflicts.

As I review my own life and career, it is astonishing how many significant relationships have been built and maintained in this manner – being somewhere in my mind and body I hadn't planned to be, by helping someone I hadn't planned to help, or being a part of something that's outside the envelope in which I normally exist. I especially remember the stepping stones placed for me by Joe Lucco, John Watson, Earl Lloyd, Ed Spencer, and Dennis Mathisen.

In an earlier chapter, I mentioned the New York Technical Tape Corporation basketball experience. Although, my primary responsibility was as a member of a National Industrial League basketball team, by becoming curious about the business and becoming acquainted with one of the company executives, I was offered a companion opportunity in their customer service department. In a sense, that seemingly simply experience was the genesis of my front office white collar business career.

SATURDAY MORNING RELATIONSHIPS

Obviously it's beneficial to become familiar with people with whom you are involved, whether they be employees, peers, customers, or superiors. How those relationships develop can be critical to success. A "Saturday morning" relationship is a phrase I use like currency at Honeywell. Harvey McKay a good friend and successful entrepreneur, lecturer and author, introduced me to the phrase. Good relationships are tested by a hypothetical Saturday morning unannounced call. How does it make you feel? What's the reaction on the other end of the phone? Test it in your mind – you'll know if the value you placed on the relationship is shared.

REAL, WIN, WORTH

My friend Dr. Norm Sidley taught me to use this caption to describe a process of evaluating relationships and opportunities. It can be applied to both business and personal life. There are three basic components:

Before we invest our valuable time, energy, and capital – we begin by asking – is this opportunity real enough(likely to happen) to merit the investment of the energy it will require? Or, does it have the odor of a pipe dream or mirage?

Secondly, can it be won? If you do all the right things, can you accomplish what you set out to do? (Is the a game or opportunity that you are capable of winning after giving your best efforts)

Finally, after you have it in hand, will it be worth having and worth the energy (remember energy is a valuable, increasingly priceless commodity).

It's amazing the number of efficiencies you discover when you evaluate opportunities in this manner. Real, win, worth.

PLAY WITHIN YOURSELF (TO YOUR STRENGTH)

Over the years, I've developed a reputation for not over-reaching, for staying within the confines of my capability, for not over-rushing, and for not being greedy. These traits can be traced to my upbringing. Grandfather Jackson emphasized the danger of wanting too out of a transaction or relationship - that the wanting often causes you to step outside your comfort zone.

To avoid this, one first must successfully determine what their skill, physical, and emotional capacities are. That doesn't mean they can't be expanded through experience and additional knowledge, but it's essential to have a feel for your capabilities at any given time. The metrics are energy, passion, intelligence, and most important time.

My father often talked about not outrunning your headlights, which is another way of putting it. "If you go beyond your field of vision," he would say, "bad things usually happen." Work on the things that increase ones field of vision.(health, experience, education and good intentions)

BE A GIVER, NOT A TAKER

This was another family-mandated value. Grandfather Jackson told me early in life that civilization is comprised of givers and takers and it was important to determine which I was going to be. Intelligence, energy, and preparations prepare you to be a giver.

There was no doubt as to his preference. "We Jacksons have always prided ourselves on being available for other people." He said. "When the world advances to a point where most of us consider ourselves givers, we'll have a much better neighborhood and world."

HAVE A POSITIVE, CAN-DO ATTITUDE

I find that a positive attitude is vital for energizing yourself and a workplace. It doesn't have to be unrealistic, but it becomes contagious.

In times of crisis, I tend to look for opportunity. My CEO at Honeywell, Ed Spencer, always stressed that a down market was the best time to invest. When competition is having problems, that's not the time to reap profits. Market share and relationships are great investments in difficult times. (think about it) The healthy neighbor who never answers the phone or door appreciates a friendly visit when their health fails.

Everyone has the ability to decide what he or she wants his or her lives to become and then design a process for reaching the desired outcome. Corporations call this visioning. In your personal life, it's simply saying you're taking control of where you'll be going as well as the outcome you desire.

Professional speakers like to say that the road to success is one that's always under construction. But first, the road you take should have a pre-designated destination.

If done thoughtfully, today you could write the resume you hope to submit ten years from now.

DEFINING AND REDEFINING SUCCESS

Once you've decide not to be a victim, but the architect of your dreams and outcome of your life, then it's important to develop realistic milestones, or success stops, that allows you to pause and make intelligent course adjustments. I recommend small steps and clearly defining each before its undertaken. Once you complete each early step, you'll be encouraged by your success.

TAKE CARE OF MIND AND BODY

This is the most vital of strategies, and no one can do it for you. The mind and body must serve you a long time and you are the only keeper of this estate. Success comes to those who have the energy both physically and intellectually, to endure. Thus, your game plan for life should include a vision of how you're going to manage yourself emotionally and how you'll maintain your body, whether it is through diet, exercise or biofeedback. Moderation and faith are essential parts of a healthy lifestyle.

LIFE REALLY IS A GAME

I have learned to approach life's situations and crises in a strategic and understated manner. One needs an ability to laugh (buy a front row seat to a Harlem Globetrotters game), to see the humorous side of things and thereby, reduce tension. Losses should be viewed as lessons that set the stage for future wins.

In business, I see each decision, not as a career-threatening burden or home run (I like singles), but as just another game to be mastered and enjoyed. Given that sense, it's amazing how much easier work becomes and how much easier it is for those who work with you.

Life is a collection of visions/dreams and tactics followed by setting realistic goals, developing alternative directions, measuring milestones, understanding the barriers, keeping myself focussed while keeping the pressure on myself and those around me as I try to be the best in class. These are also things we identify with my favorite game of basketball.

Dream Plan Book Tutorial

Congratulations! Assuming you have read the course book, and completed ***The Playbook.*** You are now prepared to write and publish your Dream Plan Book. If you haven't already started, use this tutorial to write, create, and publish your ***Dream Plan Book.***

If you haven't yet downloaded and started to put together your ***Dream Plan Book,*** this section is for you. These are *the steps in order* for building your ***Dream Plan Book,*** starting at the very beginning.

Important Getting Started Hints, Timing

Since you have done the preparatory work in ***The Playbook*** for creating your ***Dream Plan Book;*** this part will go rather quickly. Once you get started, it is going to be engaging and exciting. Therefore, if possible, start when you have an uninterrupted span of time. Starting on a Friday evening or Saturday morning, will allow optimal time for your creative focus.

• **Download Software:** Go to www.authoryourdreams.com to download the **BOOK SMART SOFTWARE.** This is where you will build your ***Dream Plan Book.*** Have login information that came with this course handy.

• **Undo Button:** The BOOK SMART software is organized similarly to WORD. Here's a helpful hint, which can save you "oodles of time." It is the **UNDO option**—it's the first item on the drop down menu of the Edit function. If you accidentally type something or hit a wrong key, immediately go to Edit at the top left, next to the File button, and click on UNDO at the top of the drop down list.

- **New Book Set Up:** Click on the BOOK SMART ICON on your desktop or Start Menu to open it. If you want more detail about the software right now, click on "Getting Started Guide." If you are ready to get started right now, click on "Start a New Book."

- **Book Title and Size:** At the top of the window, it will say, "Choose a Size," and below it will be a place to type in Book Title and Author Name. Type the name of your *Dream Plan Book,* (from the workbook play 7-1); and your name as author in the space allowed. Then choose the **square 7 x 7** size for your *Dream Plan Book.* Click on "Continue."

- **Select Layout:** The New Set Up window will say: "Choose Your Starting Point." Suggested layouts for Dream Plan Books are text & photo, portfolio, blog to book, and poetry. Click on any of those layouts to see which layout you prefer. This will depend on the amount of text versus amount and size of photos you have collected in the workbook process. You may change the layout later, so for now select a layout you like, and then click "Continue," or "Start Book Now." If you click on Start Book Now, it will open up the BOOK SMART SOFTWARE and you can start manipulating the components of your book right away.

- **Get Photos:** The New Set Up Window will say, "Get Photos." This can also be art you have scanned in and saved in your computer. All photos and artwork needs to be in a jpg format, and with a 300 dpi format. You may browse your computer for your photo files, or search for photos by going to www.freefoto.com or www.dreamstime.com. The software will give you the choice to download photos from your computer or from various photo sources. **Note:** Keep in mind that this book is just for you, and not for being marketed or sold to others. If the photo or graphic arts aren't the highest quality, and the software is shows you a "low resolution" warning message, and if it looks fine to you, ignore the warning. At this point if you click on the get started now, it will launch you to the software. Or click on "Continue" to choose a theme.

- **Choose a Theme:** You have a choice of three looks. Click on one you like and then click Continue. The cleanest, most simple one is called "viewfinder." You can change this later after you see what your photos and text look like together. Click Continue to add your title.

- **Add Your Title:** Fill in the name of your ***Dream Plan Book,*** from your workbook in Step 7-1. Click on "Add Your Book Title Here" and type in the title. At this point the Book Smart Guide has launched you into to BOOK SMART SOFTWARE. You have now created a new book, with title, a layout, theme, and photos. Next you will add your text consisting of your dream statement, your dream script, and a dream decree from Play 3-4 and 5-1; 5-2; and 5-3. Once you get these text items input into your book, you may also add additional quotes, or thoughts as your ***Dream Plan Book*** begins to take form.

- **Bring in Text:** Input your dream statement from play 3-4 at the end of the conceive section, your dream theme, dream script, and dream decree from Play 5-1, 5-2, and Play 5-3 of the believe section. You may spread it out on several pages, to complement your graphics. Add a quote for your opening page. Your may find quotes online at www.quotationspage.com; and can search by keyword for the quote you want; or take pertinent quotes from your journal, if have one; or from your favorites books.

- **Preview:** Depending on how adept you are, or how much of a perfectionist, expect the Dream Plan Book to take from 4 hours, and as long as a week to complete. Some will complete it in one sitting; others are extra creative and will make use of borders, decorations, and color options available. Looking at these options can take time. Simply use the "Preview" button on the lower right hand corner of the BOOK SMART window to see what your book will actually look like when published. Then click on "edit" to go back to your work.

- **Pages:** Use up to 40 pages in the square 7" x 7" book size. Or use as few as 5 to 10 pages, if you want to keep it simple—there is no pressure to use all 40 pages.

- **Proofing:** There are a couple things to do before ordering your final book. Run spell check, which is in the edit menu at the top of the BOOK SMART Menu. Be sure that all images or photos, and text are yours unless you have the written permission to use the work, or have given proper credit. Check fonts to be sure they are what you want—the correct size, bolded or italicized, lower or upper case. Finally, print out a hard copy proof to check it for errors.

- **Upload and Order:** To order, click on the "preview" at the bottom right of the window. Then, click on "order" in the lower right hand corner of the BOOKSMART

SOFTWARE. You will be brought to an Upload and Order Screen. Depending on the size of your file, it will take some time to upload to the publishing site. Once loaded, you will be asked to sign in with your login, password, and *physical* shipping address. Make payment with your credit card, gift card, or promo code. When your order is complete, you will see the book cover, and may scroll down to "edit book settings" to "turn on book preview." This is cool—the pages actually flip as you turn them! Click on save, and then click the book cover icon to preview the first 15 pages of your final Dream Plan Book right away. After finished loading, another screen will appear that says, "Upload Complete." Click on order and follow the instructions.

• **Backup:** Booksmart is extremely user friendly, but is not perfect. It is a very large and complex graphic arts program, that has many automated book publishing features that would otherwise take hours of learning to use. Therefore be wise. Get a flash drive and EXPORT your book to the flash drive as you do work on your book. The more photos and graphics and information you add to your book, the more vulnerable it becomes to bugs and issues inside of Booksmart. Therefore use wisdom and back up your book on a flash drive as you go along. If Booksmart crashed or you computer has issues, you can always IMPORT your book from your flash drive.

• **Privacy:** Your *Dream Plan Book* is for your personal use only. You will not be selling it or marketing it to the public. Therefore, once you have ordered and published your book, be sure the option provided in the "edit book settings" tab is set to "private."

• **Questions not covered:** *Go to www.AuthorYourDreams.com to send us an e-mail with any other questions! or e-mail us at info@AuthorYourDreams.com.*

Ten Dreams to Reality Steps

PART ONE: CONCEIVE

—**Step 1** Launch Your Courage
—**Step 2** Drive Your Desires
—**Step 3** Free Your Imagination

PART TWO: BELIEVE

—**Step 4** Stage Your Dream
—**Step 5** Pen Your Dream Script
—**Step 6** Set Your Dream on Fire

PART THREE: RECEIVE

—**Step 7** Publish Your Dream Plan Book
—**Step 8** Inspire Your Dream with Action
—**Step 9** Awaken Your Dream with Thanks

FINAL: ACHIEVE

—**Step 10** Become a Dream Achiever

Dictionary of Terms

Dreaming Muscles: The idea that the *dreams to reality* concept can be learned and developed as a skill; and strengthened with use and practice to conceive, believe, receive, and achieve a dream on purpose.

Dreams to Reality Process: The on-purpose process, from beginning to end, that propels its creator through conceiving, believing, receiving, and achieving a dream objective.

Dream Writer: A dream writer is a deliberate dreamer who creates a dream statement, script, and story to become the author of his/her own person *dream plan book*.

Dream Deniers: Those emotions, obstacles, and persons who would try to separate dream achievers from the manifestation of their dreams.

Dream Doers: Those persons who are determined to follow their dreams and make them come true!

Dream Elements: Creative graphic pieces of meaningful artwork, personal photos, quotes, thoughts, words, poetry, designs, colors, shapes, and scanned images brought together to tell the dream story in a *dream plan book*.

Dream Implementer: A dream implementer is an advanced and practiced dream writer able to dream dreams so powerful that they reach beyond their own lives and times, to create dream wealth for others.

Dream Objective: A passionately desired outcome.

Dreams to Reality Action Plan: Includes three parts: introduction to dream planning, dream planning workbook *(The Playbook),* and use of proprietary software for creating a self-published dream plan.

Dream Script: As Dream writers, we become the author of our dreams. We deliberately write a story line from which to build our dream stories, which ultimately become our published dream plan books.

Dream Statement: A simple explanation in 15 words or less, defining a vision, goal, or idea that one has decided to conceive, believe, receive, and achieve. This statement forms the basis of the dream script.

Dream Story: The narrative that a dream writer creates in preparation for writing their *dream plan book.*

Dream Plan Book: The physical outcome of the *Dreams to Reality Action Plan.* It is a 7" x 7" 10–40 page storybook, authored by the reader in the simple format of a children's storybook. It is the dream writer's illustrated, creative narrative of their defined deliberate dream objective.

Dream Theme: It is the emotional component, which emerges from the dream script to drive the dream storyline.

Dreamwealth: A concept coined by author of *Dreams to Reality* to referring to unlimited abundance expressed by the soul when united with its source. Worldly success pales in contrast to dreamwealth that yields unlimited abundance and fulfilment.

www.AuthorYourDreams.com: Membership website for Dream-writers, who intend to become the author of their dreams and their own personal *dream plan book.*

Powerful Resources

AngelArts: Dana Susan Beasley, graphic artist, publisher, writer, entrepreneur. Websites: www.angelarts.biz, www.angelartswebstore.com.

The Bible: The scripture quotes of Jesus Christ can be found in the new testament of the *Holy Bible*.

Creative Visualization, by Shakti Gawain: This is a simple and powerful book on how to activate the power of imagination and visualization in a purposeful way. Website: www.shaktigawain.com.

Do what you Love, The Money Will Follow: Marsha Sinetar, 1989, Random House. www.marshasinetar.com.

Magnificent Mind at Any Age, Dr Daniel Amen: A book about brain health and natural and preventative steps we can take to keep our brains healthy and energetic. Website: www.amenclinics.com.

Jamie Nelson Studios: Jamie Nelson, Fashion and Beauty Photographer. Website: www.jamienelson.com.

Power vs. Force, the Hidden Determinants of Human Behavior, by Dr. David Hawkins, MD., PhD: His research correlates vibration frequency measurements with states of mind and emotion. Website: www.veritaspub.com.

Psycho-Pictography: The new way to use the Miracle Power of Your Mind, By Vernon Howard: m 1965 by Parker Publishing Company, Inc. Author uses the power of word stories and parable visualization to teach the ages' greatest wisdom.

Pre-Paid Legal Services: Legal membership/insurance, and New York Stock Exchange Company, and business opportunity. Website: www.prepaidlegal.com/hub/debnelson.

Seaside Creative Services: Gwen Ellis, Editor, Author, Speaker. Website: www.gwenellis.com.

Secrets of Manifesting: Paul Bauer, Dreams Alive, website: www.dreamsalive.com.

The Astonishing Power of Gratitude, by Wes Hooper: There is a free PDF download of book at the website, www.dailygratitude.com. This book explains the power of gratitude goes beyond a spiritual principle, as it will also attract things of tremendous value into your life.

The Power of Intention, by Dr. Wayne W. Dyer, Hay House, Inc., Carlsbad, California, This book is about harnessing the power of what you strongly desire to bring it into reality. Website: www.drwaynedyer.com.

The Power of Now, by Eckhart Tolle; 1999, Namaste Publishing. This book teaches the incredible power of the present moment, and gives ways to overcome the habit of living in the past and projecting fears into the future. Website: www.eckharttolle.com.

The Science of Getting Rich, by Wallace D. Wattles: Originally published 1910, free PDF download at website, www.scienceofgettingrich.net.

The Theory of Reality: Learn Quickly and Easily How to Change Your Life and Live Your Dream! By Larry and Diana Bogartz: published by Xlibris Corporation. This is a book about faith as it relates to reality written from a scientific view. Included are great techniques for building and practicing faith. Website: www.theoryofreality.com.

The Secret: A unique, independent documentary film addressing the idea that we attract that which we focus on. Website: www.thesecret.tv.

The Way They Learn, *by Cynthia Ulrich Tobias, Focus on the Family Publishing, 1998* An informative book which addresses the unique learning styles of different types of personalities. Website: www.applest.com

The Wizard of Oz, by Frank Baum (1939). A film starring Judy Garland, about ordinary people who go on a journey from wishing to dreaming, to living their dream; they ultimately take responsibility for their desires and dreams.

What the Bleep Do We Know? Down the Rabbit Hole: A documentary of interviews with scientists and Spiritualists involved in the research of quantum physics and where reality/perception meets up with physics. Website: www.whatthebleep.com.

www.AuthorYourDreams.com: website for Dream-writers, who intend to become the author and planner of their dreams; by writing their own personal ***Dream Plan Book.*** It is a website of resources for the ***Dreams to Reality Action Plan.*** **Dream Objective:** A passionately desired outcome.

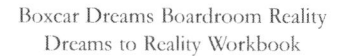

About the Author
Mannie Jackson

Mannie is currently Chairman of Boxcar Holdings, LLC a collection of business initiatives that include sports properties, real estate holdings, supply-chain management, broadway and casino entertainment ventures in which he is the managing general partner and or the majority owner.

As Chairman Owner of the Harlem Globetrotters, Mannie Jackson achieved a dramatic corporate turnaround restoring the Hall of Fame basketball team to its status as a global icon. A former Globetrotter player, Jackson purchased the team in 1993 and revived the near-bankrupt organization into one of the most admired and publicized teams in the world, while increasing revenue five-fold and rebuilding the fan base to near record levels. Before a national television audience, the team confirmed its status as one of the best and most influential basketball teams in the world when Jackson and the Globetrotters were the just the fifth team inducted into the Naismith Memorial Basketball Hall of Fame on September 27, 2002. In fact, the team was recognized a record six times in a seven year period by basketball's most prestigious barometer of success.

Jackson stepped into the history books when he purchased the team in 1993, as the first African-American to own a major international sports and entertainment organization. The conclusion of the team's 2005 North American Tour in April 2005, marked 12 consecutive years of double-digit growth. Jackson amassed an impressive list of national sponsors, expanded countries visited to 118 with attendance of over two million annually, and topped the Sports Q ratings as the most liked and recognized team in the world in 1999, 2000 and 2002. In late 2005 Jackson sold or liquidated Boxcar Holding assets valued at over 150 million dollars.

Jackson has served on the Board of Directors of si Fortune 500 companies - and has served on the Board of Governors for the American Red Cross. He is currently serving as chairman of the Naismith Memorial Basketball Hall of Fame and was among 12 distinguished nominees for the Archbishop Desmond Tutu Award for Human Rights in recognition of his work in South Africa. During the Kentucky Derby weekend celebration, Jackson was named 2005's Man-of-the-Year by the Winner's Circle for Children Inc. in Louisville, Ky. Recognizing years of promoting human rights throughout the world, The National Civil Rights Museum in Memphis, Tenn. presented their inaugural International Award to Jackson in January 2006. In July 2006, the African-American Ethnic Sports Hall of Fame in Harlem, N.Y., honored Jackson's corporate achievements with the prestigious Basketball Entrepreneur Award.

Jackson is a founding member and former president of the Executive Leadership Council, providing African-American executives with a network and leadership forum to promote excellence in business. In 2002, Jackson and the Globetrotters were inducted into the Black Sports and Entertainment Hall of Fame. This recognition was followed by the National Conference of Community and Justice's (NCCJ) Arizona region honored Jackson with the 50th Annual Humanitarian of the Year Award. Later that year, the Rainbow/Push Coalition awarded Jackson the prestigious Effa Manley Sports .

Executive-of-the-Year Award. In the spring of 2003, Lincoln University in Pennsylvania, the nation's oldest historical black college, founded in 1854, recognized Jackson with an honorary doctorate degree in Humane Letters for his work within the business community.In 2006 jackson received the Highest award presented to a former student-athlete. Jackson was also presented the Distinguished Achievement award from the Executive Leadership Council in 2003.

Prior to taking the reins of the Globetrotters in 1993, Jackson served as President and General Manager of Honeywell's Telecommunications Business before retiring as a Corporate Officer and Senior Vice President of Honeywell, Inc. Jackson has been recognized in various prominent financial publications throughout his career, including being named one of the Nation's 30 Most Powerful and Influential Black Corporate Executives; one of the Nation's Top 50 Corporate Strategists and in 1992, was named one of the 20 African-American High Net Worth Entrepreneurs. In the spring of 2001, "Harvard Business Review" published a first-person account of Jackson's business principles that turned the Globetrotters into a market leader and the most renowned sports team and entertainment entity in the world.

During the 1996 and 1997 season, Jackson and the Globetrotters were instrumental in securing over $2 million for the Nelson Mandela African Children's Foundation. From 1993 to 2005 the Globetrotters charitable contributions totaled over $15 million. In the fall of 1997, Jackson announced an endowment of $100,000 to the Lincoln School Alumni Foundation of Edwardsville, Ill., helping provide youth with college scholarships and pledged $250,000 to the Globetrotters Alumni Association. The NCCJ, which Jackson contributed $125,000 to, recently named the Harlem Globetrotters Scholarship Fund, awarded to Arizona youth, allowing them to participate in the NCCJ's leadership program, Anytown USA. During the 2001-2002 Jackson directly contributed $100,000 to the American Red Cross for the Disaster Relief Fund to help victims of Sept. 11th tragedy. In 2003, Jackson presented the Basketball Hall of Fame with a quarter of a million dollar donation to continue basketball's greatest legacy and in 2006 became the largest single donor in hall of fame history with a million dollar cash contribution. In January 2005, Jackson pledged $100,000 to UNICEF to aid victims of the tsunami in Southeast Asia, as well as a $250,000 donation to the Edwardsville, Illinois YMCA building fund. In September 2005, Jackson donated $200,000 to victims of Hurricanes Katrina and Rita in the Gulf Coast. In 2007 the Jackson family established a 2 million dollar scholarship, education, and mentoring fund for needy and deserving students attending the University of Illinois. The program is called the Mannie L. Jackson Academic Enrichment and Leadership Program.

Born in a railway boxcar in Illmo, Mo., Jackson grew up in Edwardsville, Ill., earning the title of Illinois' "Mr. Basketball," and attended the University of Illinois with high school teammate and lifelong friend Govoner Vaughn. Vaughn was named the teams MVP and with Jackson became the universities first African-American All-BigTen and All-American players. During that time, Jackson was also elected varsity captain of the Illini basketball team. He is also a charter member of the Illinois Basketball Hall of Fame, and a member of the National Black Sports and Entertainment Hall of Fame, as well as, a charter member of the Black Legends of Professional Basketball, and is an investor with a limited partnership interest in the Arizona Diamondbacks. Jackson and his wife, Cathy, reside in Las Vegas, Nev., and have two adult daughters: Cassandra, a graduate of New York University and DePaul University, and is a marketing executive in the vegetarisn and vegan food industry, and Candace, a graduate of New York University and Columbia University, is a reporter-writer for the Wall Street Journal.

About the Author
Deborah S. Nelson

Photo by Deb Halberstadt

Dreaming and Writing—What do they have in common? Perhaps it is Deborah S. Nelson—who has united her two best talents in] 3 recent book series, ***Dreams to Reality, Make it Real,*** and ***Boxcar Dreams To Boardroom Reality.***

Avid student of motivational materials spanning decades, Nelson has thrown her hat into the self help venue with a simplified neurolinguistic coaching process which uniquely creates a self-published book as the outcome of the learning.

And Nelson practices what she teaches and preaches. The author's first big dream, at 14, was to become a newspaper editor and writer. And she fulfilled that dream early on, within her first year of junior high school.

Her next dream was to fund her college education. In love with writing, between studies and work she made time to write for her college newspaper. Dreaming and writing, she graduated in the '70s, debt free, with a BS from the University of Texas. Soon after, she joined *The Austin Sun,* a weekly entertainment and cultural magazine.

In the '80s, Ms. Nelson emerged from a dramatic divorce in the role of *solo parent*. This challenge created just one thing for Nelson, a new dream—to raise her daughter as a happy, healthy, successful person, rather than as a statistic of a broken home.

Concern for her child's future propelled her into a new era and a new dream—to start one of American's first "home-based businesses," with a $2500 investment in a personal computer in 1996. That dream realized offered her the freedom to become a full-time, *on-purpose, solo mom.*

Eventually, Nelson was able to fund most of her daughter's education at Brooks Institute of Photography, her daughter's dream college! Her daughter is a successful independent fashion and beauty photographer, following her dreams all over the world shooting for fashion magazines.

Devoted to women in business, Nelson was recognized by *Working Women Magazine* in the '90s for entrepreneurial excellence; and selected as a national finalist for Ms. Corporate America 2008—another childhood dream realized.

Ms. Nelson is an author/entrepreneur, running a boutique publishing company, and has founded Author Your Dreams, Author Your Book, The AdStuff Company, The Dating Passport, Vacation Rental Gurus, Haiti UP!, and Reality Based Coaching System. Author of 9 published books, she splits her time as a Publishing Coach and Dream Coach, teaching Dreams to Reality and Author your Book Courses. She is in the process of writing and publishing 2 books to be available in 2011, a true story, *Oops, I Married a Con Artist,* and *New Branding Secrets for the Solo Entrepreneur.*

In the **Dreams to Reality Action Plan,** a synthesis of 25 years of study, reading, and life experience, Nelson masterfully merges two recurring themes—her love of writing, and her ability to set dreams in motion. In symphony with Mannie Jackson, Nelson offers transformational *10 Dreams to Reality Steps* in the **Box Car Dreams to Boardroom Reality Playbook**, as the reader walks the exciting *dreams to reality* autobiography of Mannie Jackson. With 9 published books under her belt now, what is her next big dream? It is to teach millions of readers how to make their dreams come true on purpose!

Other Books By Nelson:

Dreams to Reality: *Introduction to Dream Planning*
Dreams to Reality: *Author Your Dreams Workbook*
Dreams to Reality: *Author Your Career Workbook*
Dreams to Reality: *Author Your Book Workbook*
Vacation Rental Owner's Manual: *Do it Yourself Vacation Rental Management*
Make it Real: *Reality Based Coaching, Part One: Textbook*
Make it Real: *Reality Based Coaching, Part Two: Workbook*
Bain Moves to the Beach, *From Mountain Dog to Beach Dog*

Photo Album

Photo Album

Boxcar Dreams Boardroom Reality
Dreams to Reality Workbook

www.BoxcarDreams.com

Photo Album

All Rights Reserved

Boxcar Dreams to Boardroom Reality

199

Photo Album

Boxcar Dreams Boardroom Reality
Dreams to Reality Workbook

www.BoxcarDreams.com

Photo Album

All Rights Reserved   Boxcar Dreams to Boardroom Reality   201

Photo Album

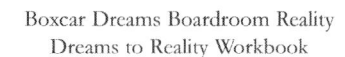

Notes:

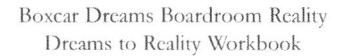

Notes:

Made in the USA
Charleston, SC
10 April 2012